Motivating Your Organization

SERIES EDITOR
BARRIE DALE
UMIST

Motivating Your Organization

ACHIEVING BUSINESS SUCCESS THROUGH REWARD AND RECOGNITION

Colin Pitts

McGRAW-HILL BOOK COMPANY
London · New York · St Louis · San Francisco · Auckland
Bogotá · Caracas · Lisbon · Madrid · Mexico · Milan
Montreal · New Delhi · Panama · Paris · San Juan
São Paulo · Singapore · Sydney · Tokyo · Toronto

Published by
McGRAW-HILL Book Company Europe
Shoppenhangers Road, Maidenhead, Berkshire SL6 2QL, England
Telephone: 01628 23432
Fax: 01628 770224

British Library Cataloguing in Publication Data
Pitts, Colin
  Motivating Your Organization: Achieving
  Business Success Through Reward and
  Recognition. – (Quality in Action
  Series)
  I. Title II. Series
  658.314

ISBN 0-07-707967-1

Library of Congress Cataloging-in-Publication Data
Pitts, Colin
   Motivating your organization: achieving business success through reward and recognition / Colin Pitts.
     p.   cm. – (Quality in action)
   Includes bibliographical references and index.
   ISBN 0-07-707967-1
   1. Compensation management. 2. Employee motivation. I. Title.
   II. Series: Quality in action (London, England)
   HF5549.5.C67P53   1995
   658.3'14–dc20   95-1427
                                                                                  CIP

Copyright © 1995 McGraw-Hill International (UK) Limited. All rights reserved. No part of this publication may be reproduced, stored in a retrieval system, or transmitted, in any form or by any means, electronic, mechanical, photocopying, recording, or otherwise, without the prior permission of McGraw-Hill International (UK) Limited.

12345 BL 998765

Typeset by BookEns Ltd., Royston, Herts.
Printed and bound in Great Britain by Biddles Ltd., Guildford, Surrey.

Printed on permanent paper in compliance with ISO Standard 9706.

Contents

Series Preface		vii
About the Series Editor		xi
Introduction		xiii
1	**Motivation** Inherent motivation • A sense of achievement • Social attitudes • Culture change • Goals • Pay as a motivator	1
2	**Reward or recognition?** Definitions • Why do we need reward and recognition? • Reward and recognition as agents for change • Reward or recognition?	13
3	**Individuals or teams?** Individuals • Teams • Teams in the ascendant • Summary	20
4	**Options for recognition** Recognition for teams and individuals • Recognition for individuals only • Corporate recognition • Relationship of recognition to reward • Summary	33
5	**Application of recognition in practice** Culture • Peer group selection • Starting out • Avoiding oversight • Corporate awards • Concluding remarks	45
6	**Suggestion schemes** Suggestion schemes vs TQM • Synergies with TQM • Case study • Threats and opportunities • Suggestion schemes within TQM • The future • Summary	56

7	**Options for reward**	66

Reward, pay and value • Pay as a motivator • Targets for reward • Basic pay • Basic pay plus income improvers • Basic pay plus results-based increments • Basic pay plus status symbols • Basic pay plus long-term benefits • Differentials • Summary

8	**Performance-related rewards**	82

Who judges the performance? • Individuals or teams? • What performance? • How can performance be defined and measured? • Is it fair? • Is the reward committed or results dependent? • Who allocates PRP? • What will it cost? • PRP and TQM • Solutions • Summary

9	**Application of reward in practice**	93

Setting basic pay • Income improvers • Appraisal • Results-based increments • The overall reward package • Summary

10	**Measures of performance**	111

Progress of the TQ process • Outputs • Inputs • Metrics • Goal setting • Behaviour • Other soft issues • Appraisal procedure • Basic rules of performance measurement • Summary

11	**Leading on learning and nurturing knowledge**	152

Dynamic systems and interaction • Continuous learning and essential competencies • Some practical aspects of continuous learning • Boffins are beautiful, specialists are special • Rewarding skill • Leading on learning • Concluding remarks

12	**The future**	160

The total quality continuum • The place for reward and recognition • The fruits of reward • Future structures • Behaviour • Ownership and membership • The reward package of the future • It is all about recognition • Final thought

References	179
Index	182

Series Preface

Quality is regarded by most producers, customers and consumers as more important than ever before in their manufacturing, service and purchasing strategies. If you doubt this just think of the unsatisfactory examples of quality you have personally experienced, the bad feelings it gave you, the resulting actions you took and the people you told about the experience and the outcome. The concept of Total Quality Management (TQM) is increasingly being adopted by organizations as the means of satisfying the needs and expectations of their customers.

Total quality management has been practised by the major Japanese manufacturing companies for the last 30 or so years. Their commitment to continuous and company-wide quality improvement has provided them with the foundation by which they have been able to capture markets the world over. In response to this competitive pressure Western manufacturing companies, first in America and then Europe started to embrace the TQM ethic; this was followed by commercial and service-type organizations. The superior performing Western organizations have now some 15 or so years of operating experience of TQM.

Total quality management is a subject and management philosophy in which there appears to be an unquenchable thirst for knowledge, despite the considerable volume of published material. The objective of this major 'Quality in Action' book series is to help satisfy this need and fill what we believe are gaps in the existing range of current books. It is also obvious from the arguments advanced from some quarters that there is still a lack of understanding of TQM and what it is about. Hopefully the books in the series will help to improve the level of understanding.

SERIES PREFACE

McGraw-Hill has already published books by three of the best known and internationally respected quality management experts – Crosby, Feigenbaum and Juran. The 'Quality in Action' series will build upon the work of these three men; this in itself will be a challenge.

I was honoured when asked by McGraw-Hill to be the 'Quality in Action' book series editor. I have personally been involved in industrially based TQM research for the last twelve or so years and from this experience believe I am well placed to identify the aspects of TQM which need to be addressed by new books on the subject.

The prime focus of the series is management and the texts have been prepared from this standpoint. However, undergraduate and postgraduate students will also find the books of considerable benefit in understanding the concept, principles, elements and practices of TQM, the associated quality management systems, tools and techniques, the means of introducing, developing and sustaining TQM and the associated difficulties.

One objective of the series is to provide some general TQM reading as guidance for management in introducing, developing and sustaining a process of continuous and company-wide quality improvement. It will focus on manufacturing, commercial and service situations. We are looking for recognized writers (academics, consultants and practitioners) who will be able to address the subject from a European perspective. The books appearing on this theme will not duplicate already published material, rather they will build upon, enhance and develop the TQM wisdom and address the subject from a new perspective. A second objective is to provide texts on aspects of TQM not adequately covered by current books. For example, TQM and human resources, sustaining TQM, TQM: corporate culture and organizational change, partnership sourcing, TQM and business strategy. It is likely that the authors of these books will be from disciplines (e.g. accounting, economic, psychology, human resources) not traditionally associated with quality management. A third objective is to provide texts which deal with quality management systems, tools and techniques in a practical 'how-to' manner.

● SERIES PREFACE

My commitment to this series is that I am prepared to allocate time from my considerable research, teaching and advisory activities in order to ensure that it meets and hopefully exceeds the needs and expectations of our readers.

B. G. Dale, Series Editor

About the Series Editor

Dr Barrie Dale is Reader and Director of the UMIST Quality Management Centre. The Centre is involved in three major activities: research into Total Quality Management (TQM); the Centre houses the Ford Motor Company Northern Regional Centre for training suppliers in Statistical Process Control; and the operation of a Total Quality Management Multi-Company Teaching Programme involving, at any one time, eight collaborators from a variety of industrial and business environments. He also coordinates the Bowater Corrugated Division Total Quality Performance Multi-Institute Teaching Programme. Dr Dale is also a Non-Executive Director of Manchester Circuits Ltd, a company specializing in the manufacture of high technology and complex printed circuit boards.

He is co-editor of the *International Journal of Quality and Reliability Management*, now in its eleventh volume. Dr Dale is co-author of *Managing Quality, Quality Costing, Quality Improvement Through Standards, Total Quality and Human Resources: An Executive Guide* and *The Road to Quality* and has published over 180 papers on the subject of quality management. Dr Dale has also led four missions to Japan of European executives to study the application of TQM in major Japanese manufacturing organizations.

Introduction

The first thing I must tell the reader is that I am not a personnel specialist or any sort of an expert on reward and recognition, but that I write from the standpoint of an operating manager in a UK-based, international chemical company with a strong manufacturing base. From this vantage point I have enjoyed and endured the processes of culture change for over six years. Most of this time, including the previous 20-plus years, I have spent close to the production front line. The vehicle for these changes in culture has been Total Quality (TQ) and the book assumes a simple working knowledge of this process.

The large multi-national company that was my professional home for many years embarked on its TQ road in 1987 and used the Philip Crosby organization to get started. Philip Crosby had become an established guru of the TQ movement with an international reputation. His thinking was based on the simple idea that quality was defined as the adherence to the customer's requirements. This definition formed the first of four 'absolutes' that were at the heart of the process. The second held that the system for achieving quality was prevention; the third that the only standard was zero defects and finally, that the measure of success would be the price of non-conformance. These aside, the strong cultural message is that everyone could be and should be involved by always striving to improve what he or she did. He outlined 14 steps to achieve his vision of a quality culture, one of which was recognition. I received my initial training in TQ from them and went on myself to train many other colleagues at all levels of the organization. We eventually produced our own approach to the process and my most formative experience has been as a line manager observing the practice of TQ.

INTRODUCTION

All of this left me sufficiently unscathed to take on the corporate responsibility for the implementation of TQ and quality systems.

The opinions that I express in the book are my own and do not represent those of any former employer or any other organization. They have been forged in the light of my experiences and I will illustrate them liberally from this source. However, I will also refer to my understanding of practice in industry at large.

Having seen a TQ process put in place, and its relationship to human behaviour, I know the importance of any activity that impacts on our motivation, and key among these activities are reward and recognition.

Colin Pitts

Motivation

CHAPTER 1

Before getting too deeply into my subject of reward and recognition, I believe it will help if I discuss my understanding of what makes people want to work.

At its simplest level we work because we have to in order to earn a living to support ourselves and our dependants. So reward or pay may have something to do with motivation; in fact the word 'reward' is better because it implies a degree of recognition. But why do we do the particular work that we do? Assuming that we have a choice, the answer is perhaps because it is available locally, we have the appropriate skills, the conditions are congenial and we find some satisfaction and stimulation in doing it.

INHERENT MOTIVATION

In these times of recession that we have experienced in the 1980s and 1990s, we all know somebody who cannot get work or who has suffered the shock of redundancy, and in them we can see that there is more to work than just earning a living. The pain that they suffer has to do with their dignity, their ability to make a contribution, their membership of a team with a purpose, and the opportunities for achievement that work gives us. The experts say that a feeling of self-worth ranks high in the scale of motivation; reward and recognition are highly geared reinforcers of that feeling. Kerry Napuk (1993), writing on business strategy, says ' ... teams and employees who "feel good" about themselves can accomplish much ... Positivism and morale are powerful forces ... .'

In my view nobody comes to work to do a bad job. We all share a natural inclination to seek satisfaction from a job well done. That satisfaction will vary according to the skills of the worker and his or her perception of the object of the work. Does it contribute to an understandable, relevant and credible goal?

Some of the most difficult people that I have had to manage have been those whose skills and aspirations have gone unfulfilled and unrecognized. Their frustration has been brought to bear on their work and they have been uncooperative, idle and even disruptive. The solution, of course, is to give such individuals something more demanding to do, but in the old order of things that would mean promoting them – and that could not be done, as how could we be seen to be rewarding such adverse behaviour? One particular shift operator fitted this description perfectly; he had been with us for 10 years and had progressed as far as he could up the operator skills hierarchy without too much difficulty. Now he was blocked by the pyramid effect; there were not often vacancies for senior operators. His performance over the next couple of years deteriorated until he was becoming a nuisance to his colleagues and his supervisors. Careful interviewing revealed that here was an intelligent man who ran a successful business on the side at home, who contributed to the life of his community in several ways and who had a wealth of ideas of how the operation of the plant could be improved. When he was recommended for promotion to supervisor there was intense opposition from my colleagues and his peers alike. In time he became a very accomplished supervisor.

One of the challenges to any culture change process is to release the ideas, energies and enthusiasms of all employees at all levels of an organization, to liberate their inherent motivation to do a good job and to register achievement. Reward and recognition reinforces their achievement and helps to add value, the value of their heads as well as their hands.

A SENSE OF ACHIEVEMENT

Some of us have been privileged enough to pass our working lives enjoying the jobs that we have done; we have enjoyed them because they provided us with a platform for achievement, we have been able to make a worthwhile contribution and have been stimulated as well. Is this a privilege that should only be accorded to those who have been able to follow a chosen career? Or is it rather a responsibility of managers to create conditions wherein anyone has a chance to enjoy what they do? Robert Ford, Personnel Director at AT&T developed this principle in the 1960s, setting out to enrich jobs in order to motivate the people doing them (Ford, 1969). This principle is being applied today and will continue to be developed through multi-skilling and whole job ownership (see Chapters 7, 9 and 11).

SOCIAL ATTITUDES

In the 30 years that I have been an observer, social attitudes to work have changed. There was a time when to be seen to cooperate with 'management' was some sort of class betrayal. In this atmosphere there was no route to capture the knowledge, experience and pride in a job well done of the majority of the workforce; if enlightened employers wanted to tap into some of their ideas they had to create a suggestion scheme (see Chapter 6); in those days suggestions would be about things to be done or provided by management, not about work practices. In this environment an individual's motivation was to maintain his standing among his workmates. He would not embarrass them by offering work practices that were better than a norm which had somehow been set collectively to protect the weakest – the lowest common denominator. This was an absolute barrier to any sort of change. These attitudes had been fostered by management as much as by organized labour. There had been a philosophy of pay rather than reward based on ' ... as little as you can get away with ...' which was countered by restrictive practices, condition money, overtime and so on. It was only the oddball who was prepared to be a social pariah, at least at work, who would try to break out of this stand-off.

3

After what has seemed to be very slow, often painful change over the years, now in many companies there is a much more open environment. It has been realized that the expert on any job is the person doing it and his or her ideas for improvement are not only welcome but vital if continuous improvement is to be sustained. As behaviours change, and the perceived threat of peer competition diminishes, attitudes change towards social acceptability.

CULTURE CHANGE

Any change of culture within an organization has certain common features: it must be planned, it must be led and managed from the top, it must have a clear purpose of improvement and it must be organization-wide. As the change of culture progresses there are three other essential elements (Fig. 1.1); it will have to have some sort of change process and there will also have to be a change in the behaviour of its employees but, inevitably, it will also have to alter its structures. These three elements, process, behaviour and structure, have to be worked in parallel; but how do these elements of change impact on motivation?

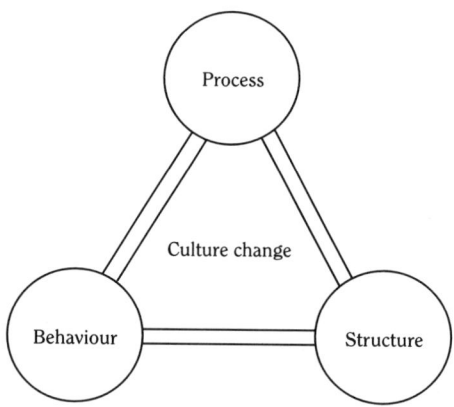

FIGURE 1.1   Culture change

Process

The introduction of a process dedicated to change the way an organization conducts its affairs, to change the concepts that drive it and to change its focus, is likely to have some sort of effect on the people of the organization. Pent-up energy, enthusiasm and determination, frustrated till now by conformity to accepted norms, will be released. The very idea that change is OK, that ideas are not just acceptable but needed, will motivate people at all levels in an organization.

I have seen people who have worked for 20 years on the same manufacturing plant suddenly produce a flow of ideas, solutions to long-standing problems, ingenious innovations, all in just a few months, once they realized that the change process was in fact real. Previously, if at all, they had advanced their ideas through a suggestion scheme which had constrained the flow through the inertia of its own bureaucracy.

When new process values become an established fact, when prevention at the root cause level is actually addressed and there is a practical concern to satisfy the customer, then the prospect of genuinely improving everyday work becomes a reality. And when these concepts are reinforced by the recognition given by managers, then the process is likely to endure – it is creating its own motivation.

A large new manufacturing facility, a multi-million pound investment, had started up after a lot of hard work and protracted problem solving at the commissioning phase. There had been a huge shared motivation to get the plant started, which had been rewarded by success. After a few months' operation, things began to go wrong and the plant was having to shut down quite often. The problem would be fixed and the plant would restart; this persisted for many more months until the plant's unreliability became an embarrassment. A new manager was appointed whose first action was to tell staff that the plant was designed to operate continuously and that was what it was going to do. He discovered that they were rating their own success and achievement by the ingenuity and speed in overcoming the plant shutdowns. He changed the perception of the process from one of 'get restarted as soon as possible' to 'don't shut down'. This simple change from 'fix-it' to 'prevention' motivated the staff to look for the causes of unreliability and to deal with them. Within six months the plant had regained an acceptable level of reliability.

It had been a feature of the process industry in which I worked that we had been excellent fixers, good 'fire fighters', the best crisis managers. All our technical skills and ingenuity, tremendous commitment, long hours and dogged determination would be applied to overcome problems that had occurred – to climb out of holes once we had fallen into them. What is more, this culture was reinforced by reward and recognition: this was the way to get noticed and it often produced personal letters of commendation from an eminent name, or even a bonus! Meantime the plant that ran quietly and reliably, producing month in, month out, received no accolades at all.

I have said that most staff would be motivated by a process of change, but there are those who have won and maintained their position by their knowledge and practice of the established way. They have often built up their status within this environment over 20 or more years; to be told now that there is a new and better way is certainly not motivating and will be seen as a threat. Many of these people are to be found in the ranks of the middle and front-line managers. Small wonder that it is not uncommon to find that this is where the most significant barriers to the change process are to be found.

Behaviour

Changes in behavioural atmosphere motivate others to get involved in the change process and to modify their own behaviour. Open behaviour can become infectious, so those who are not prepared to embrace it should not implant the germ. It is particularly virulent among the young. They come to us naturally open, they are keen to make a personal impact and if the eager are empowered, their motivation will be released and you need to be prepared to manage the output of all that energy. If you ask them to network with others, do not be surprised when their information is better than yours. Peter Scott-Morgan, an associate director of consultants, Arthur D. Little, asserts that many culture change initiatives falter because managers fail to take account of the hidden networks that really make things happen, what he calls the 'unwritten rules of the game' (Scott-Morgan, 1994). It has been said that it is much more difficult to lead in an open, empowered organization than to manage in a command and control hierarchy; some of us have found that out to our cost.

It is an interesting exercise to hand empowerment top-down through an organization because as soon as it hits a level where it really impacts on motivation, it bounces back, bottom-up, making all sorts of new and challenging demands on leadership. The ultimate test for a leader wanting to know how this new situation is being handled is to introduce some formal upward appraisal (see Chapter 10). This is guaranteed to focus the mind and may even give motivation.

Structure

Any culture change requires an appropriate structure in which the process of change can operate effectively. New organizational structures can have a powerful impact on motivation, and often a powerful negative impact. This is true when structural change is forced by, for example, the successive downturns in the economic cycle in the early 1980s and 1990s which focused attention on all parts of the cost make-up. In commodity industries in particular, price pressures became irresistible and new and inventive ways of attacking the cost base had to be found – the motivation of survival at its crudest.

Manpower costs were a rich source of saving, even in industries such as the chemical industry with low labour intensity. Couple this pressure with the culture change imperative to reduce layers of management and some impressive results have been achieved. BP Chemicals reduced manpower by 3000 in the 1980s and 5000 between 1989 and 1993 and there are numerous other examples from all sectors.

Productivity, cost reduction, cost improvement, rationalization, downsizing, rightsizing, restructuring, re-engineering are all terms that are used: the effect is to reduce the numbers employed. That means that real people no longer have work in the organization; people with hopes, aspirations, career plans, loyal people, dedicated, committed people, competent people suddenly realize that the world has taken an unpleasant turn for them. How can it be possible to maintain motivation in these circumstances?

When large numbers of people are going from an organization it is not possible to avoid a general feeling of depression, but there are three critical requirements. First, those that have to go deserve to be treated in a civilized, sensitive and as generous a way as can be achieved. Second, the organization must retain its credibility as a 'quality' operation for those that remain. The method of handling the painful reductions is key and the decisions must have wide acceptance – be understood and endorsed by as large a cross-section as possible. Finally, it is vital that the new reduced structure is seen to have removed the old barriers to improvement, so that the remaining people can rekindle their motivation through empowerment and team work.

So organizations have to change their structures as part of culture change and that has an impact on motivation. In the old hierarchies, the constant striving to achieve the next status level was a potent force for motivation. But if the hierarchy is not dead it is seriously wounded. Flatter organizations with less managerial layers arise from the need for shorter, simpler and more precise lines of communication; and empowerment removes much of the need for control and second-guessing. They also mean less steps on the ladder, less opportunities for promotion and hence less motivation from the prospect of promotion. So if motivation is to be maintained the new structures have to afford new opportunities: to be part of an effective team, to register achievement, to make a full contribution and to be recognized and rewarded.

Job for life

There is a dying form of motivation that has something to do with long-term loyalty. It could be described as 'keep your nose clean, toe the line and give due deference to your elders and betters, and you may get to the top of the tree in 20 or 30 years'. Though common in some successful companies, in Japan for instance, where it is often linked to a reliable pay-by-age policy, this approach has always seemed to me to have more to do with the intimidation to conform than with motivation. For sure, it will become a historical curiosity and will not feature in the future when there is unlikely to be such a thing as a job for life, perhaps even in Japan.

GOALS

I have shown how I believe the three elements of culture change can influence motivation. I now turn to discuss what is, in my view, the single most powerful motivator. It is a basic requirement of all effective work that it can be related to some reputable goal. If the object of the exercise is obscure, how can anyone generate enthusiasm to work for it? The TQ approach to policy deployment rests on that simple contention – define the objectives and translate them into relevant goals at all levels of the organization.

The corporation will set out its strategic goals. The constituent businesses will interpret them with their own strategies, and these in turn will transpose into the goals of the operating units, teams and ultimately individuals (Fig. 1.2). The policy deployment process must be transparent so that anyone can readily grasp their own goals expressed in the appropriate language but can also make the connection to team goals, business

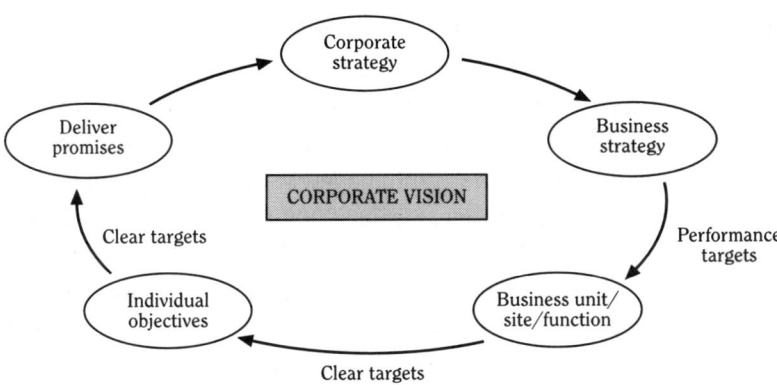

FIGURE 1.2   Policy deployment

objectives and corporate strategies – so that when they hear the company chairman holding forth, or a business chief executive, or their own team leader, they can relate it to their own work and put their contribution in context.

The test that this process is working effectively is when there is feedback. When there is sensible comment bottom-up on the shape and working of the corporate strategy, then the process is working.

As well as a clear understanding of strategy and objectives, it is important that the framework of values and the ultimate vision of the company are understood. They must be part of the corporate knowledge. The reputation of an organization is a fragile asset; lessen the controls and it is more at risk. When empowered individuals or teams are taking decisions, they must be in no doubt about the values that influence their judgement. Similarly, no goal, objective or strategy can be in conflict with the corporate values or threaten the corporate reputation.

I visited a manufacturing site recently and asked a middle manager what the goals of his team were and how they related to the business strategy. He reached into the bottom drawer of his desk and took out a six-page document of close typescript; he proudly assured me that 'it was all in there!' Asked if each member of his team understood them he said, 'Oh yes, they all have a copy of this'. I persisted and asked which extract from the document came to mind when they faced work on a Monday morning, and at this he began to be a little less comfortable.

By contrast, a newly appointed business chief executive who wished to make a fresh start with his team set a business objective that simply said 'Reduce costs by £10 per tonne'. Within a few weeks it was possible to ask anyone at any level in that business (some 2000 people) what the objective was and '£10 per tonne' they would reply. The punchline is that the objective was achieved in nine months. Then of course they had to search for a new objective, and it was interesting to observe from outside as the consensus for 'Another £10 per tonne' rapidly developed. The simpler the goal, the more relevant it will be to more people, and hence more effective will be the communication.

Other companies have achieved incredible motivation for improvement using stretched or outrageous targets. The Motorola Corporation, for example, had its vision of six-sigma quality and successive annual targets that called for, not percentage increases, but tenfold increases in performance levels, and achieved them. They have no doubt about the motivating effects of goal setting.

PAY AS A MOTIVATOR

Of the benefits received in return for performing the tasks or service we call work, pay is the most significant. Those who have from time to time taken part in some form of management training will, no doubt, have been asked to make a list of motivators at some time. I expect that few would put pay at the top of the list but most will have included it somewhere. There are other things we work for, many of them I have discussed above, but at its most fundamental it is pay that moves us to go out and seek work of some kind.

To some, however, pay (i.e. wages and salary) is not a motivator but a 'hygiene' or 'environmental' factor. It contributes to the environment in which we are prepared to work, it sets the context in which we seek to achieve, and is often a measure of that achievement. There are many models that try to capture the stimulae of motivation such as Maslow's 'Hierarchy of human needs' (Maslow, 1954) and Herzberg's 'Two factor theory' (Herzberg *et al.*, 1959). But to my mind this debate is not worth carrying too far; if pay sets the stage on which employees are prepared to strive to achieve, then it qualifies as a motivator. Pay sets a mutually acceptable common value to the individual's contribution. For sure it can be a powerful demotivator – when the reward package has been poorly constructed the negative affect is obvious. James Creelman when he was editor of *TQM Magazine* put it succinctly: 'Whether we like it or not, a major motivator for the vast majority of people attending a place of work is the money they receive at the end of the month, or week' (Creelman, 1992).

Therefore my inexpert view is that pay is a motivator. If employees are uncomfortable with the reward package, and pay is the largest part of this, then all of the other motivating factors discussed in this chapter will be ineffective. Dale and Cooper (1992), writing on TQ and human resources, list 16 common management failings: among them they note the failure to recognize and reward individuals and teams, observing that reward and recognition are key motivators.

CHAPTER 2

Reward or recognition?

DEFINITIONS

My definitions of reward and recognition are as follows:

- Reward: the benefits that arise from performing a task, rendering a service or discharging a responsibility. For employees who have contracted to perform these duties on a regular basis, the principal reward is pay. However, it is not quite that simple, for many employers do not simply offer wages or salaries but a 'reward package' of which wages and salaries are a part. The package may typically include:
  - bonuses
  - pension schemes
  - health insurance
  - allocated cars
  - mortgage assistance
  - beneficial loans
  - subsidized meals
  - profit sharing
  - share schemes
  - share options

  and so on. For a complete list, the best source is probably the income tax authorities who wage an ongoing campaign to ensure that these benefits are not tax-free.

- Recognition: the demonstration of appreciation for a level of performance, an achievement or a contribution to an objective. It can be confidential or public, casual or formal. It is always in addition to pay.

In general terms, reward is the pay and recognition is the handshake.

Why do we need reward and recognition?

The argument surrounding the need for both reward and recognition harks back to the question of pay as a motivator. It is a universal recognition of relative worth. As you see, it becomes impossible to progress this discussion without having to use one 'R' word to describe the other! So why do we complicate the issue by adding this apparently separate concept of recognition? It goes back again to motivation; we like to achieve, we like to share that achievement with others and have it recognized and celebrated. When this need is satisfied, then it is motivating. This motivation only works if that recognition is likely to be forthcoming.

Reward alone

If we were to rely on reward alone to recognize contribution and achievement, there is a danger that the objective may become modified to one that is to secure the pay and nothing more, i.e. to get to the end of the week or the shift, to 'keep your nose clean' and that is all. This will degrade the culture of the organization. We would sink into the worst excesses of doing as little as we can get away with, to demarcation and all the other horrors of restrictive practices that were at their height in the 1960s and 1970s.

I remember one day walking past a fitter who was leaning against a door post of the plant workshop; around his feet was a collection of valves awaiting service and overhaul. I said, cheerily, 'What's up with you, Jim, have you nothing to do?'

'Oh yes,' he said, 'I'm on these valves.'

'Why don't you get on with them?' I asked, a little more tetchily.

'Because they are down there and my work bench is in there ... I've asked the foreman to get a labourer to move them,' he said in triumph. His achievement was to pass as much time as possible without actually doing anything.

The industrial culture of the time encouraged this sort of attitude; on the trade union's part the philosophy was that all members were equal and did equal work of equal worth – it was management's job to get adequate value from that work. In this regime individual recognition was anathema. Of course, management's response was often equally crude, always giving as little as it could get away with. Even in the non-union professional and staff ranks, recognition bore the stigma of the 'blue-eyed boy'. For me one of the great achievements of the total quality movement of the 1980s was the idea of the improvement ethic. It was good to do work as well as it could be done and that recognition for special performance was acceptable.

For these reasons I believe that reward alone is not enough. Recognition is not just a matter of style, something that some individual managers use, a matter of luck whether or not you get the chance to be a recipient. Recognition is part of the culture and an essential complement to the reward system.

Reward, a necessary evil – recognition, a blessing?

I do not want to give the impression that recognition has some sort of cultural purity about it that sets it above other forms of motivation. Also I have never understood the contention that you must not use cash as a means of recognition. Certainly in BP Chemicals the policy was no cash when recognition began to be officially encouraged. We shall return to this in Chapter 4.

The same view that invests recognition with a form of ethical superiority often casts reward as a necessary evil. Perhaps we should only work for the satisfaction provided by doing work well, and allow our employer to provide directly for our essential needs, housing, food, clothing, etc. Far-fetched? Well, employers do get involved in these areas more than we may think: not only the obvious examples from the turn of the century, when industrial benefactors built Port Sunlight and Bourneville for their workers, but today how many provide subsidized or free meals, clothing, health care and pensions? However, even William Lever and Thomas

Cadbury paid their workers a decent wage to which all other benefits were an addition.

Money is our measure of value and we all need a value set on our work. We need to feel that the activity that will consume 30 per cent of our waking existence is worthwhile. More fundamentally, in modern economies, we have to earn a living.

Value for money

Since we have to be paid for the work that we do, we might as well use our pay systems to maximum advantage. As pay is so crucial to the support of our loves and lifestyle, we quite naturally compare what we receive with others. So concepts of fairness and status are intrinsically bound up with pay. It is emotive and thus potentially dangerous. It is fundamental to the relationship between employer and employee. If we get it wrong we will demotivate immediately and strongly. Pay policy and practice also convey messages and it is important that they are consistent with the cultural thrust of the organization.

Performance and promotion

There are those who believe that reward and recognition come together neatly at the point of promotion and that this is as far as recognition need go. For these the motivation is in the promise or the hope of promotion, the drive of ambition. As organizations become flatter, opportunities for promotion reduce, but in fact they only ever applied to a minority of employees. The motivation of the prospect and fact of promotion can only be sustained for a comparatively short period before and after the event, yet the negative effect of disappointment can be long lasting and insidious. For these reasons it is a mistake to rely on promotion as a means to recognize and reward performance.

Links to success

There is a strong argument to link all reward and recognition to success in an ongoing way. I for one need my appetite for reward and my thirst for recognition satisfied more frequently than the prospect of promotion every three or four years or longer, if the vigour and enthusiasm of my performance is not to decline.

There are risks in linking reward to success associated with its antithesis, namely failure. What if someone actually fails in the job? If his reward package is linked to success, we are forced to face up to the situation and take remedial action rather than to live with it. What if the job is performed at the minimum acceptable level with no obvious success? Again we will be forced to acknowledge that situation and search for new ways to define success in this case. The subject of performance-related reward is contentious and will be dealt with in detail in Chapter 8.

REWARD AND RECOGNITION AS AGENTS FOR CHANGE

Chapter 1 put forward my belief that no change in culture will occur unless there is a change in behaviour. If people do not actually alter the way that they do things, then nothing will happen. I also believe that one's attitudes, including attitudes to work, are formed as a result of emotional influences. Therefore to alter those attitudes, to change the paradigm, we have to impact at the emotional level. Reward and recognition both work at this emotional level and so will have an impact on culture and culture change. They will have that impact whether or not we manage it, so if we wish to use these powerful levers to enhance the change process we need to get control of them and set them in the correct position. Failure to align them will be an impenetrable barrier to culture change.

The culture change process in BP Chemicals stalled in just this way about two years after they had introduced the TQ process. They had made 18 000 people across the company aware of the principles; they had installed structures in which the process could work and develop; they had provided a range of tools and techniques to allow everyone at their own level to improve what they were doing, yet nothing much happened! Why? After some soul-searching they concluded that the missing element was behaviour and that they would correct this at first by concentrating on those with some form of leadership role. This view had been supported by the near failure of their work groups in some places. These were groups of people who normally worked together; the groups had been set up in order to discuss ways in which they might make improvements. Their leaders were front-line supervisors, foremen and the like, and were totally out of their depth when it came to getting sensible and valuable output from these groups. If is added to this fraught scenario reward and recognition based on the success of these groups, there arises a dilemma that threatens the credibility of the TQ process. On the one hand the company wanted to encourage this sort of activity by properly aligned deployment of reward and recognition; on the other hand, this would add anxiety, even fear for their income, to the discomfort that supervisors were experiencing in these new situations.

There was an almost audible sigh of relief when the company introduced behavioural training for leaders; it was an instant success. The emotional impact of the linkage to reward and recognition contributed in no small measure.

REWARD OR RECOGNITION?

I have argued that recognition is a powerful cost-effective way of enhancing the improvement process and an essential adjunct to culture change. It enables people to feel involved and it creates a positive atmosphere in which success is allowed and differentiation is not a threat, in which it is all right to achieve. Its impact, though immediate, will endure.

With regard to reward, I have suggested that as well as pay policies being applied to create a value environment in which work is done, such policies also have a strong supporting role for the TQ or culture change process. Pay has a high potential for negative messages and therefore must be crafted carefully to yield maximum advantage (these matters will be addressed in more depth later in the book). By its nature pay cannot be changed frequently and changes in pay themselves have relatively short-term impact; it is more important that in creating a context for work the pay policy must be seen to value the visions and goals of the improvement culture. It must reward those that are recognized as progressing towards the vision, achieving the goals, and changing their behaviour.

Reward and recognition both have a place in enhancing the TQ process, they are complementary and the impact of one would be reduced without the other. As in all aspects of management it is a question of balance; but I am certain that both systems must appear to have been born of the same beliefs, to be part of the same philosophy. This is not as easy as it looks because recognition is a matter for interpretation by the local manager while pay systems are worked out by a central personnel function. But it is none the less true that they must be aligned and this is a test or reality check for the dispersion of the TQ process throughout the organization.

CHAPTER 3

Individuals or teams?

The initial response to any suggestion concerning reward and recognition is to consider how it affects 'me', the individual. This should not necessarily mean that 'I' cannot be rewarded and recognized as a team member as well as an individual. Charles Handy (1994) describes what he calls 'the Paradox of the Individual': in the late 1980s the right to pursue private success was a driving principle of politics (certainly in the UK and US) and yet there is an assumption that anyone who matters is part of a company, organization or group, and represents them rather than themselves. The paradox also exists in reward and recognition and it is worthwhile examining it.

INDIVIDUALS

Good reward and recognition is essential to motivate individuals to perform to their maximum potential and to take advantage of the leverage that healthy rivalry can provide. But there are dangers.

1 *Personal agendas.* The most significant danger is associated with personal agendas. All of us have these and they may or may not coincide with the corporate strategy or team goals, but when push comes to shove it will be the personal agenda that comes into play irrespective of its effect on the corporate or team interest. A site manager refuses all pleas

to release one of his staff to another job in the company for which he is seen to be the best candidate, because he perceives that such a move would weaken his own position. This sort of defending of the power base and turf wars are all examples of personal agendas in play.

2 *Innovation unrestrained.* A concern of the 1990s, when empowerment is the order of the day, is that we will need some way of setting boundaries to unrestrained individual innovation and enterprise. There must be a clearly defined framework of parameters and values within which the empowered individual can work. This can be difficult to achieve on an individual basis.

3 *Short-termism.* Individual rewards mean individual targets and objectives. These will be set annually, and the ambitious will be determined to achieve them at any price. He or she will be sure to achieve the ends, whatever the means. This can positively act against long-term strategies, continuous improvement, visions and values. All of this is in direct conflict with total quality. There are some scenarios which encourage this sort of behaviour. For example, when the financial performance is poor and the imperative becomes survival, the politically aware manager will accept very tough cost reduction targets with little or no consideration for the longer-term impact. I have seen basic preventive maintenance being cut in just such a situation only to see plant reliability suffer two or three years later. Conversely in a boom situation, output at any price is the cry and costs are added without concern for the legacy of the cost burden in leaner times.

These are extreme cases but we do need to be aware of the dangers if we are to successfully manage individual reward systems. There are some techniques which go a long way to help.

- Policy deployment: this has been described in Chapter 1 but is important as a counter to short-termism and private agendas. Individual objectives are positively linked to longer term business or corporate strategies.
- Appraisal: this a formal way of reviewing progress against objectives and will be dealt with in detail in Chapter 10.
- Job tenure: we should try to leave people in post for longer periods so that they experience the long-term impact of their short-term approach;

in this respect a two-year stint is hardly sensible, even for high fliers.
- Reward and recognition: as I have said before, the way that reward and recognition are used sends messages. The message must be to endorse the required behaviour and to reject personal agendas and short-termism.

There will always be the need to recognize and reward individual performance, and the dangers of individualism can be countered, but the most effective way is the greater emphasis on teams and team work.

Teams

Barriers

Reward and recognition of teams is a subject that provokes the usual defensive arguments for the status quo, all the familiar barriers to change:

'It may work elsewhere, but it wouldn't suit our culture ...'
'Nice idea, but too difficult in practice ...'
'Reward is a private matter, this threatens privacy ...'
'High performers will be held back ...'
'People often belong to more than one team, how can we handle that? ...'
'This is a flavour of the month ...'
'Will this improve the bottom line tomorrow? ...'
'No more new initiatives please ...'
'Let's leave it to local management ...'
'It will be disruptive ...'
'The time is not ripe. ...', etc.

It is because the concept seems to threaten the mechanism with which we assess our own value that these arguments are deployed with such vigour.

The importance of teams

Team learning is one of the five disciplines in Peter Senge's influential book *The Fifth Discipline* (1992) in which he sets out the art and practice of the 'learning organization'. He defines it as '... aligning and developing the capacity of a team to create the results its members truly desire'. He further asserts that individual learning is irrelevant to organizational learning, while team learning provides the microcosm for learning throughout the organization. Jon Katzenbach and Douglas Smith (1993a) stress the importance of distinguishing between teams and work groups; work groups may be teams if they have been properly formed up but they do not become an effective team simply by giving them that title. Katzenbach and Smith say that teams are differentiated by having mutual accountability, team purpose, collective outputs, open-ended discussion and problem solving, by working together, not individually, and by being judged on the team output.

Our own experience, too, tells us of the inescapable importance of teams; the modern industrial and commercial world requires the effective combination of so many different skills and activities for a successful outcome that it is hard to understand how that could be achieved without the use of teams. Certainly nearly everything worthwhile that I have achieved in my life in manufacturing industry has been as part of a team. In the 1960s, when TQM was but a gleam in someone's eye, I was fortunate to be part of a commissioning team. This team spent six months working towards a common goal: to get a major investment in new plant up and running on time and making product successfully. It was hard, sometimes frustrating and constantly challenging work. The team included engineers of all disciplines, foremen from widespread backgrounds, craftsmen and plant process operators, many of whom were completely new to their jobs, literally recruited off the streets – butchers, bakers and candlestick makers.

The outcome was that the plant started on the appointed day and ran successfully first time. As a personal achievement, that ranks as one of the most satisfying in 30 years, and yet it was not mine – it was the team's, but I was part of it!

The hidden assumption

One of the basic claims of TQ is that it provides a vehicle to involve anyone at all in striving for excellence; it reverses the old hidden assumption that people below a certain level in the hierarchy had no heads (Fig. 3.1).

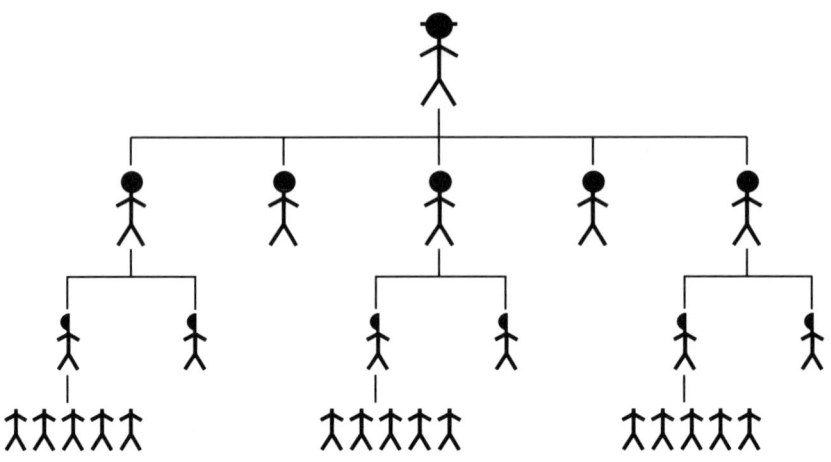

FIGURE 3.1 The hidden assumption

The only sensible arrangement for achieving such a reversal is to organize people in teams. This is not such a revolutionary idea as it may sound. After all, people have always been organized into departments, sections, groups, shifts, etc. What has been added is an understanding of team dynamics and the importance of the mix of skills and the constructive resolution of conflict within the team. Professor Edward Lawler of the Graduate School of Business Administration in the University of Southern California notes that quality circles were devised because we did not organize normal work groups as effective teams (Lawler, 1992); as we learn the benefits of doing this, so the need for special groups such as quality circles diminishes. When the new behaviours of trust and openness are introduced together with common goals and focused leadership, then we have a group of people working effectively together. All of their energies and talents can combine to give an output that is greater than the most effective combination of their individual outputs. Now, if we organize so that these teams work in a flat empowered structure, we shall release their full potential. We will have recognized that everyone has heads.

Leadership of teams

Most erstwhile managers and supervisors who have taken on the role of a team leader will admit that they have found it to be much harder work than in the old hierarchical management regime. It is much harder to facilitate and guide the work of an empowered team than to direct and control subordinates. But this is a culture change and therefore the leader's behaviour must change. A change from:
- telling to listening
- imposition to encouragement
- defending to supporting
- instructing to coaching
- directing to delegating
- blame to recognition.

In much of the industrial and commercial community these are traumatic changes but I know of none who have made the transition who would want to revert to the old ways because it is such a satisfying way of working. In many of the stronger developments of teamworking the role of the leader changes so significantly that the team becomes 'self-managed', that is, the team does not seek a leader appointed from outside but is confident to arrange its own leadership internally, often appointing different leaders for different tasks or projects.

Teams and TQM

Teams create an environment in which so many of the principles of TQM can be seen to be in play. They are usually small enough (often 8 to 12 strong) for the team's goals and customers to be clearly identified as well as the process to satisfy those customers. There is a desire created for continuous improvement through continuous learning, and the individual skills and aptitudes of individual members can be effectively harnessed thus each individual is more likely to feel satisfied with his/her contribution. Teams promote ownership of work and that puts them at the heart of the TQ process.

Reward and recognition in teams

Given that teams have become and are likely to remain an important feature of the working scene, how does this affect reward and recognition? Let us look at some analogies. Figure 3.2 is an illustration of one that originated from Wallace Co. Inc. in the USA.

There is plenty of allusion to motivation and recognition and even reward in this piece, and there are many other examples we could choose: herds of elephants, schools of whales, troops of monkeys, etc. However attractive the natural history analogies are, perhaps a more down-to-earth example is required. Most of us, when we think of teams, think of sporting teams of some sort, football, rugby, hockey, basketball or whatever. In any of these there is a wealth of individual talent and these individuals will have strong personal agendas. But they know that they can only realize those agendas through the vehicle of the team performance and team success.

The successful team:
- is strongly led
- has clearly understood objectives
- the members are coached and learn together
- works together every day
- has developed their own tactics
- its members are all accountable for the results.

In terms of reward and recognition, it is quite likely that team members will have reward packages reflecting their individual skills, experience and value to the team. This does not cause problems within the team; they understand that the team is a mix of talents which will attract different rewards. Bonuses are paid to recognize particular team achievements and to individuals for notable performance. Recognition is immediate and obvious both for the team and individuals. As well as cups and medals, there may be media exposure and endorsements, and the member of a successful team enhances his or her own reputation and value by association and has that 'reward' or self-satisfaction of having been a member of the 'A' team. More than this, the organization of which the team is part will often adopt a systematic approach to recognition by nominating a 'man of the match' or 'player of the month or the year'.

● INDIVIDUALS OR TEAMS?

FIGURE 3.2 Geese in formation (author's drawing after an idea by Wallace Co Inc.)

When geese
travel in formation,
they travel about 70 per
cent faster than when they fly alone.
Geese share leadership. When the lead
goose tires he (or she) rotates back into the
'V' and another flies forward to become the leader.
Geese keep company with the fallen. When a sick or weak
goose drops out of the flight formation, at least one other goose
joins to help and protect.
By being part of a team, we too can accomplish much more, much faster.
Words of encouragement and support (honking from behind) help inspire and
energize those in the front lines, helping them keep pace in spite of the day-to-day
pressures and fatigue.
The next time you see a formation of geese, remember that it is a reward, a challenge,
and a privilege to be a contributing member of a team.

Despite all of this being part of our everyday experience, there is still a reluctance in industry and commerce to embrace the concept of teamworking so completely for it to be quite natural to apply reward and recognition based on team performance or individual performance within teams. There are of course some significant exceptions to this damning statement. Japanese investment in UK industry has brought with it their well-developed team practices and this has had influence outside the directly owned subsidiaries of Nissan, Toyota, Honda, Sumitomo Rubber and others. For example Rover, Lucas, Rolls-Royce and Vickers are well down this road and others such as British Airways, British Telecom and British Oxygen have all got good examples. The European Quality Award winner of 1992, Rank Xerox, lists teamwork and leadership through quality as two of the vital criteria in the assessment of managers. Yet still the broad statement made above seems to hold true in much of our economy. BP Chemicals may be typical of this: it had well-developed reward and recognition systems for individuals which could have been equally well applied to the team situation but many of the barriers referred to earlier were brought into play against this idea. It was left to the more intrepid local managers to use the existing systems in this more enlightened way, and a few did, but most were reluctant to take such a 'risk'. I also noted a reluctance to recognize the normal work group as a team, although many of them are just that and would benefit from being rewarded and recognized as such.

Reward and recognition in any team format

Teams can take more than one form; they can be the normal group in which one works or a task force set up to address a particular problem, they can be a shift team responsible for a particular time span or the manufacturing 'cell' coming into favour in the engineering and assembly industries, they can be mixed-discipline or cross-functional, peer-grouped or diagonally sliced. Whatever the format, the arguments for team reward and recognition hold good. If we accept the benefits of teamworking and wish that to be the preferred culture we must align our reward and recognition with that aim. This does not exclude the recognition and reward of the individual but simply requires it to be done in the context of the individual's membership of the team.

TEAMS IN THE ASCENDANT

There will be bottom-up pressure for the universal application of reward and recognition to teams as more and more people are asked to work in that format. As they are expected to display good team behaviours and to work through their personal aspirations in the context of the team, so they will ask how these efforts are to be rewarded. They will expect to see them openly and obviously endorsed by the reward system and by the style of recognition.

These pressures will ultimately be responded to and will serve to drag the reactionary manager screaming and shouting into a more enlightened era. This will, in turn, put pressure on corporate human resources departments to produce corporate policies and guidance. Pilot studies and research will be conducted and the resulting proposals will be picked over from the board downwards. The barrier cries of 'too difficult', 'too disruptive', 'too early', 'too differentiating' will be heard echoing around the corridors of power. Hopefully, meantime, the enlightened manager is using his or her empowerment intelligently to reward teams using the current systems.

Like any other aspect of change and the improvement process, uncompromising leadership from the top is necessary if the benefits of team reward and recognition are to be felt universally and promptly.

Katzenbach and Smith (1993b) define teams as small groups of people with complementary skills, committed to a common purpose, a set of common performance goals and a common accountability for achieving those goals. One of the ways they cite to build team performance is to 'exploit the power of positive feed-back, recognition and reward'. They do not suggest that this is the only or even the first thing that must be done; they believe that a significant element of reward is the shared satisfaction that comes from team achievement. I would agree with that but would add that if formal and informal recognition is not applied to the achievements of teams, and reward systems are not aligned to performance of teams and of individuals within teams, then the potential of teamworking will be inhibited.

Both teams and individuals must be recognized and rewarded. Individual contribution and achievement will always have a place and, indeed, in some situations will be more appropriate than teamwork; a balanced, thinking approach is required. Michael Armstrong, prolific writer on reward matters, observes that '... it is necessary to avoid defining individual performance in a way which is so internally competitive that it disrupts teamwork. On the other hand situations in which poor individual performance can be hidden within the team, should be avoided' (Armstrong, 1993). Individuals will need to be able to identify the recognition of their personal contribution and reward for their own achievement. But most individuals will be able to commit to the right team and to share the responsibility for its performance. In which case they will rightly expect to share in the recognition that the team should receive and identify part of their reward on the basis of the team's achievements. Finally, part of their reward should clearly endorse those behaviours that contribute to the smooth operation of their teams.

Teamworking is necessary in most situations to allow people to be at their most productive, but that does not mean that we need to, or should, stifle individuality. Human beings are social animals, they naturally interact with others in small groups, and when these groups have a shared purpose they will improve the performance of every other member of the group. This is an observed natural phenomenon; when it occurs in our work life, let us react to it, reward and recognize it naturally, rather than treating it as some alien new age concept.

SUMMARY

1 Individuals
- Healthy rivalry and dangers
  - personal agendas will override corporate strategies and team goals
  - unrestrained innovation – clearly defined parameters and values needed

- short-termism.
- Helpful techniques
  - policy deployment
  - appraisal
  - extended job-tenure
  - reward and recognition.

2 Teams
- Barriers to reward and recognition for teams
- Importance of teams
  - a learning environment
  - effective combination of diverse skills and activities for successful outcome.
- Hidden assumption
  - only the top of the hierarchy can think – TQ reverses that assumption
  - teams make it happen through team dynamics, mix of skills, constructive resolution of conflict, empowerment.
- Team leadership
  - more demanding than command and control
  - needs behaviour change
  - ultimate teams are self-managed.
- Teams and TQM
  - healthy environment for the principles of TQM
  - continuous improvement, clear goals, customer focus, ownership.
- Reward and recognition in teams
  - analogies from nature and sport
  - reluctance in the world of work
  - some positive exceptions
  - still an eccentricity in many companies.
- Application to any team format
  - teams take more than one form
  - reward and recognition applies to each
  - align with cultural aims.

3 The ascendant team

- Bottom-up pressure.
- Need for uncompromising top-down support.
- Team satisfaction is rewarding but lack of reward and recognition will inhibit.
- Teams and individuals must be rewarded.
- Treat it as a natural response to a natural phenomenon.

Options for recognition

Recognition is an accepted part of the fabric of life almost irrespective of the differences in regional cultures. It is good to give and receive appreciation and this is done in all aspects of human society. In many fields it is the natural consequence of achievement – trophies, medals, gifts and sometimes cash prizes are the norm in sport; they start with the youngest novices and carry through to the top professional echelons. All over the world academic achievement is marked by certificates, prizes, diplomas and degrees, often presented with impressive public ceremony. In national life most countries have developed some form of recognition to mark achievement or service of the highest national significance; in the UK this takes the form of medals, orders, knighthoods and peerages. Recognition is deployed in professions, societies, religious movements, youth organizations, in fact in any situation that people come together to share common interests or purpose.

The exception is the world of work, where for many recognition has not been a common event. There are exceptions that prove the rule but, in general, attempts to recognize have been rare and awkward and used only sparingly. Why should it be that this most common of all human associations is so different from all other fields? I can only believe that it has to do with the culture – the relationships that exist in this environment. Perhaps it comes from the old master–servant relationship that has persisted from the early agrarian economies, through the industrial revolution, and still echoing down our command-and-control hierarchies of today. It is not surprising, therefore, that the practice of recognition is a constituent element of the culture change routes put forward in the last decade, including TQM; because if we are to enjoy the benefits of recognition, it does imply a change in typical workplace behaviours.

Yet as we know from the world outside work, the giving of recognition is so easy to do and is great value for effort. The regional culture barrier is one that is often raised: '... that sort of thing may be all right for the USA, but it won't work here!' This is to confuse the form of recognition with the fact, and it is the fact of recognition that matters. The arguments about regional styles of recognition are often overstated too. The presentation of mugs and T-shirts has become totally acceptable in the UK, whereas a few years ago they were in the '... won't work here' class.

I will now describe some of the common forms of recognition and will recall some of the thoughts of Chapter 3 in looking first at those that are applicable to both teams and individuals.

RECOGNITION FOR TEAMS AND INDIVIDUALS

Casual

First and most important are the casual forms of recognition. These are heavily dependent on management style; the simple word of appreciation dropped into a conversation will achieve enormous motivation. So too will the more deliberate meeting in the work place especially to commend – 'I wanted to come over to have a word with you to say how much I enjoyed that piece of work you did last week. I think it will be quite significant, good work, thanks very much'.

Managers and leaders should give all members of their teams and work groups positive strokes reasonably regularly. This does not mean that criticism cannot be offered at all, but it is much more likely to be received as constructive if the context of support and encouragement has been set by regular casual recognition. This all sounds very simple and obvious, but it often takes a positive step change in behaviour for a manager to make it happen. It goes without saying that he or she will have to practice MBWA (management by walking about); you cannot have a casual conversation with your team members by calling them into your office.

Casual recognition is the most important, because if there is not an environment, a management style, in which recognition is a normal feature, any more formal form will be hollow and devalued. It is one of those difficult leadership skills and behaviours that is necessary to master in order to support our colleagues in empowered teams and work groups.

Commendation

This is one step removed from the casual. It can be private or public, written or verbal, but it is formal recognition of a particular achievement. It can take the form of an office interview, a letter with copies on personal files, or public commendation at a meeting with publicity given to the work or result with care being taken to attribute it to those responsible. Attribution is itself an effective form of recognition and costs nothing. If a senior staff member is presenting work done on his or her behalf, it is important and effective to attribute it by name to those who actually did the work. Visible signs of commendation such as insignia or badges are used effectively in some situations. Some companies have learned these methods from the military.

Publications

In a similar vein, considerable kudos will accrue and hence motivation result from the publication of papers in learned journals, professional or trade publications; similarly, presentations at public seminars and conferences are effective. Incidentally the company's reputation will be enhanced by these techniques as well.

Journalism is a good vehicle for recognition, particularly reports of successes in house journals or site news-sheets; but accurate reporting is essential if negative impact is to be avoided. You can be sure to get accurate reporting and maximum recognition if one of the team members actually writes the article.

Tokens

Apparently one of the most difficult areas of recognition in practice is that involving some physical token – a gift or memento. The golden rule is to use whatever seems appropriate and works in the local situation. There is no point in presenting recipients with gifts if they are going to be ridiculed by their peers. It must fit the local culture and have credibility in the workplace. There is an infinite range of possibilities, from T-shirts and diaries, pens and calculators to lunches or dinners with the boss, theatre tickets, sporting events, outings or visits to other sites, customers or suppliers, and so on.

Here I should discuss the question of cash as a means of recognition. I am not one of those who has a doctrinal objection to using cash as a token – in fact, by-the-event bonuses are just that and have been used for as long as I can remember. There are some problems in that it is often not credible to give relatively small amounts of cash, nor is it reasonable to give large amounts; it also attracts the attention of the tax authorities. If you can live with those difficulties then you should apply the rule – is it appropriate? Will it work?

Workplace privileges

A good example of a workplace privilege is a recipient being allocated a privileged parking space for a month. I heard of one site that had used this method to recognize someone who was not a car owner; however there was no comment from anyone when he proudly and purposefully placed his bicycle in this parking place every day for a month. Other forms of privilege are, for example, first-class travel for a period, attendance at a senior meeting that the recipient would not normally attend, etc.

Celebration

Recognition can easily and often should turn into celebration. A good outcome, a target surpassed, the best result yet, record production, record profit, all these and many more deserve to be celebrated. These celebrations, too, can take many forms: open days for families and friends always go well, quality days specifically to celebrate the progress of the quality process have been successful, and commissioning parties for all those involved in getting a plant started or restarted after a shut-down are well received. There are numerous ingenious examples of celebration events: a boat trip on the canal, a day at the races, a weekend at a hotel or country club. It always adds extra spice to these events if it is known that the boss of the business has been prepared to provide the money for the festivities from his own budget.

It is important to invite the correct population to these events or negative motivation will ensue. For example, if a big jamboree is organized for a product launch, it is important that all those involved in the successful development are invited or at least represented. Also, if shift workers are involved, things must be arranged so that no one is left out – if this means having multiple events, so be it, it will still be good value.

Implementation of suggestions

Employees make suggestions about their work, whether via formal suggestion schemes (see Chapter 6), corrective action systems, quality circles, work groups, teams or just in casual conversation. It is very motivating to see these suggestions adopted promptly. It is a practical recognition of their contribution and a demonstration of active listening by their managers or team leaders. The recognition can be enhanced by commendation, publicity and celebration as appropriate.

Structured regular mechanisms

More and more organizations are employing regular structured mechanisms of recognition. A survey conducted across 140 US firms published in 1992 (Troy, 1992) revealed that of the 115 who practised TQM, 96 had some form of formal recognition programme. With these mechanisms, recognition is always on the agenda – it is written into the calendar. Typically, a department or team will have a monthly reward – 'The Quality Achievement of the Month' or some such title, by which someone or some team will be selected, recognized and publicized. Similarly, each quarter,

the site or location or functional group, will select a quarterly award winner and at corporate level there will be an annual award – the Chairman's Award – presented with due ceremony at headquarters. I call this technique a 'hierarchy of acclaim'. It has several benefits:
- It creates an environment in which recognition is acceptable and in which the other options mentioned above can flourish.
- It allows teams/departments to put themselves on the map in corporate terms and all members of the team can bathe in the reflected glory.
- It uses the beneficial aspects of competition as a motivator.
- It creates a uniformity of approach (a standard).
- It ensures management involvement throughout the organization.

There are detractors, those who say it would not fit their culture and would be counter-productive. These arguments can usually be translated as 'too difficult' or 'I don't want to be involved' or 'I'm frightened of public comparison'. My view is that there are very few cases in which these structured mechanisms are not useful, but they should never be the only form of recognition, all the other forms must be used as well.

Recognition for individuals only

There are some forms of recognition that really only work for individuals. All of them are only effective if used sparingly, but when used like this can have very good results.

Personal skills

It can be very motivating to give individuals the opportunity to demonstrate their personal skills in a wider arena than their normal work group. For example, the presentation of work in person to senior figures (the board or executive committee perhaps). Alternatively, individuals could be nominated to represent the team at some event, function, seminar or workshop and occasionally to deputize for the team leader. Those with specialized skills can be asked to assist or coach in other work groups.

Promotion

Some would say that the ultimate in individual recognition is promotion. In some companies it has been the only form of recognition. As a motivator how effective is it? Clearly it will be restricted to the able, so that middle-of-the-road people will be left out and will be increasingly frustrated by the lack of promotion. Even the able will be more motivated by the anticipation of promotion than by the fact because shortly after the event the motivational elation will soon be replaced by feelings that it was long overdue. Finally, if it is used alone it represents the management style that I have called 'management by intimidation' – if you do not do as I want, you will not get on!

What is it that promotion recognizes – past achievement or future potential? Hopefully both and more besides: the promoted employee should be seen as a role model for the preferred culture.

In our flatter, non-hierarchial organizations of the future, promotion to another step on the ladder will be a rare event. The means of setting levels of pay will have to reflect elements other than status, but I will discuss this in later chapters.

CORPORATE RECOGNITION

The desire for recognition is also evident in the body corporate: companies and organizations believe that there is benefit in external recognition for the level of excellence that they have attained. This has been true for many years in fields like business achievement and safety performance, but it has now become an important driver in total quality.

Advantages

Most see a double advantage to corporate recognition:
- External: the publicity that attends the award enhances reputation and provides some competitive advantage.
- Internal: the challenging effort to win the award unifies the organization in a shared goal, with strong committed leadership from the top down. It

gives a focus for the formation of teams. It puts the necessary cultural changes at the very heart of corporate activities. It introduces the concept of measurement and self-assessment and focuses learning. It produces tangible evidence of progress in the quality process. And it validates the practice of recognition itself.

Standards and systems

A long-standing form of corporate recognition has been provided by those national and international bodies concerned with getting acceptable standards for the specification of products and services. These bodies usually enjoy quasi-official status and high reputations, examples are the British Standards Institute (BSI) in the UK, the American National Standards Institute (ANSI) in the US and internationally the International Standards Organization (ISO). In the mid-1980s the call for Quality Assurance (QA) started to be heard. Customers were asserting that they wished to be assured that their suppliers could provide their specified requirements consistently. BSI responded by creating BS 5750 (BSI, 1987), a 'standard' that registered the management system that assured the development, manufacture and/or supply of the product or service. The achievement of the standard was recognized by a certificate. Registration to this standard in many sectors in the UK quickly became not only a competitive advantage but a competitive necessity. The use of the standard spread rapidly into Europe and it was adopted by ISO as the ISO 9000 series. It is now gaining acceptance in the US and Canada, and other countries internationally.

This is recognition of the existence and maintenance of a management system only, and says no more about the quality culture of the organization. That is not to say that it is incompatible with the TQ process – in fact, it can be a useful vehicle to begin the quality journey, but it is only part of the story. It has been estimated that registration to ISO 9000 is worth about 25 per cent of the Baldridge Award (see below). The important feature about QA standards is that the advantage to an organization of this recognition depends entirely upon the way it is used. If it is used to promote customer satisfaction and improvement through the Deming Plan–Do–Check–Act cycle, then it can bring ongoing benefits, but if it is used as a badge on the wall, it will be a costly ornament.

A need satisfied

To be consistent, an organization that is seeking corporate recognition must be exercising a thriving policy of recognition of its own teams and individuals. For this reason, awards have become popular and have proliferated. The best known are, perhaps, The Deming Prize (especially in Japan), The Malcolm Baldridge National Quality Award (MBNQA) (for US organizations only) and in Europe the European Quality Award (EQA). There are numerous others, both national and local, for instance the Canadian Award for Business Excellence, the British Quality Award, the Excelsior Award (New York State), and many others. This idea of motivating organizations to improvement through recognition is still growing; one of the latest examples is the UK government's universal application to the public service sector of its 'Citizen's Charter' and the associated award 'Charter Mark'.

Dangers

As well as the advantages set out above, there are some dangers. The first concerns standards. If the awards are to provide genuine motivation at the corporate level they must be really worth winning in terms of prestige, and this implies that they must have demanding standards, as indeed many of them do. This can give an impression of unattainable exclusivity to a large majority of 'ordinary' companies. This majority is tending to use the award assessment models as self-assessment tools and in this way there is a trickle-down effect from the award standards. The alternative of lowering standards to make the awards more universal is the slippery slope to the 'badge on the wall'.

The second danger arises from the first. Because of the high standards, to stand a chance of winning requires an enormous commitment of resources, time and enthusiasm throughout an organization. The single-minded deployment of all this effort, of course, produces some very positive results, especially for the change process; but it can detract from the prosecution of the key business processes (see Chapter 10). This effect will be most marked in the period of anticlimax when the award adjudications are complete and the celebrations are over.

Relationship of Recognition to Reward

Alignment is the watchword. There should be no disconnection between recognition policies and practice and reward systems. It is important that both levers are seen to be working to endorse the same behaviours and the same performance. Clearly teams and individuals that have received recognition would expect to see that referred to in annual appraisals with commensurate reward.

Summary

I have discussed the following options for recognition in this chapter:
1 For individuals and teams
- Casual
    - appreciative conversation
    - positive strokes
    - management style – MBWA
    - support in empowered situations.
- Commendation
    - private and public
    - written or verbal
    - attribution
    - publicity.
- Publications
    - paper publication
    - presentation at public seminars, conferences, etc.
    - journalism.

● OPTIONS FOR RECOGNITION

- Tokens
  - gifts and mementoes
  - lunches or dinner with the boss
  - theatre tickets
  - sporting events
  - outings and visits
  - cash award.
- Workplace privileges
  - parking
  - travel
  - attendance at senior meetings.
- Celebrations
  - open days
  - quality days
  - commissioning parties
  - business sponsored events
  - product launches.
- Regular structured mechanisms
  - monthly, quarterly, annual
  - hierarchy of acclaim.

2 For individuals only
- Personal skills
  - presentation of work to senior figures
  - representing team
  - deputizing for team leader
- Promotion

3 Corporate recognition
- Advantages
  - external: reputation and competitive advantage
  - internal: cultural and validating recognition.
- Standards and systems
  - recognition for QA
  - BS 5750/ISO 9000
  - possible starting point for quality process e.g. 25 per cent of MBNQA.

- A need satisfied
  - popularity and proliferation of awards (best known: the Deming Prize, MBNQA and EQA).
- Dangers
  - dilemma of high standards and exclusivity versus universality and meaningless awards
  - use of award models for self-assessment
  - the huge effort required can detract from key business processes.

Recognition is an effective, cheap, and highly geared way of motivating individuals and teams. All of the above techniques are simple to apply. Can you afford to ignore them?

CHAPTER 5

Application of recognition in practice

CULTURE

Any difficulties in applying recognition in practice are almost always due to those cultural barriers described earlier. We have seen that a culture is characterized as the processes carried out, the structure in which the processes operate and the necessary behaviours to allow people to carry out the processes.

1 *Processes*. If the processes have been well defined with clear outputs and measures of performance, there will be a good basis for recognition.
2 *Structures*. If structures have been arranged to allow the processes to run smoothly, there should be no barrier to recognition; but if vertical 'silo' management (functional management) is still dominant, rather than a horizontal process management structure, then it will be more difficult to align any recognition with the key process objectives rather than narrow functional objectives. For example, if a business objective is to increase customer satisfaction by being able to respond to orders within three days, a production department objective is to improve reliability by having regular six-monthly maintenance shut-downs lasting a week, and management accounts have a goal of reducing product stocks, it seems that these three departmental (vertical) objectives may be incompatible. Recognition can still be applied in each department but it is not seen to

be enhancing the key business process and, in fact, directs attention away from it.
3 *Behaviours*. If behaviours do not change, then these will present the most formidable barrier to recognition. A relevant question to ask here may be whether recognition is about corporate culture or individual style? Corporate culture provides the framework within which individual styles are allowed to flourish or are discouraged. Of course we will always need different individual styles, but the range of styles that is acceptable is defined by the corporate culture; my contention is that an individual style that cannot include recognition is unacceptable.

Similarly, the corporate culture creates the environment for the recipients. When I hear that recognition is not widely used because the recipients would be embarrassed by it, I know that the corporate culture is wrong, because it is against that context that recognition is embarrassing.

Middle managers

As with many other cultural shifts, focusing on the application of recognition is often resisted most within the ranks of middle management. There is little mystery about this – middle managers are exposed in the engine-room of change, they are the ones who really have to make it happen by changing what they do. They have achieved their positions by mastering the skills and behaviours of the old order: it is what they are good at. If we now start to change the rules, obviously they will feel threatened. What is more, their standing within their peer group is put at risk as some of their colleagues adopt the new ways more quickly than they do.

One such middle manager I knew became an enthusiast for TQM and consequently began to use recognition in all its forms with good effect. When his production group achieved record production or reliability, he would take them out for beer and sandwiches, and would recognize the 'quality' person of the month with a gift and so on. This seemed fine until some people in a neighbouring production group in the same factory began to notice and complained to their manager that they were not getting beer and sandwiches, gifts, etc. Now there were two things the second manager could have done; he could have said that if his team achieved the same sort of performance he would recognize them in a similar way, or he could have complained about his managerial colleague causing discontent and disruption. Regrettably he did the latter and his superior asked that in future all planned recognition should have his prior approval. This story is an illustration of how threatening some managers find a simple change such as the use of recognition. It also provides examples of good, bad and worse. Good in that the TQM enthusiast was making recognition work for him, bad in that his example was not seen as best practice to be emulated, and worse in that the corporate culture in the factory had not changed enough to support the necessary behaviours.

Management style

At all levels the style of managing characterized by the way managers conduct themselves has to change in order to use the power of recognition. It must change in the same way as that needed for effective leadership in empowered environments and for the successful progress of TQM (as referred to in Chapter 3). As illustrated in Fig. 5.1, change from:

- telling to listening
- imposition to encouragement
- defending to supporting
- instructing to coaching
- directing to delegating
- blame to recognition

These behaviours can be seen as positively supporting TQ's continuous improvement cycle (plan–do–check–act) known as the Deming cycle (Deming, 1982), and it is important that they are all present as features of 'the way we do things around here'. Then recognition will be seen as an intimate part of the culture. It will be easy to adopt and highly geared in terms of value.

PEER GROUP SELECTION

Continuing the theme of overcoming barriers, acceptability is readily increased by adopting a system of peer group selection. When a successful

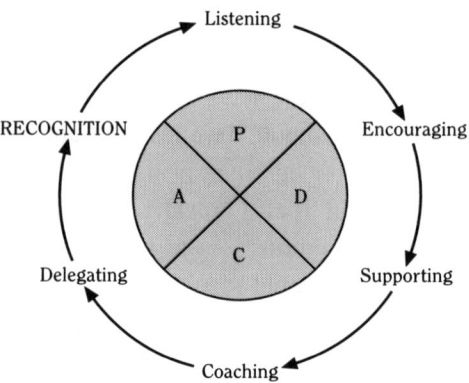

FIGURE 5.1 Effective use of recognition: a model of behaviour

recipient is chosen by his or her own workmates there can be no suggestion of 'blue-eyed boy' or boss's favourite. Also, through involvement, ownership is created and, once there is ownership, recognition will be even more relevant and effective.

Some French colleagues of mine pioneered 'Le Club des Meilleurs' to which those few per cent of people seen to be making the most contribution to improvement activity are elected by their peers. The club has several events a year, lunches, dinners, outings, etc. Membership lasts for two to three years and is seen to be properly prestigious. There are many similar examples in which a 'quality person' of the month is selected and celebrated by election from their work group as a whole or by a quality improvement team representing the work group. In these cases recognition is typically by posting a photograph of the selected person on a special noticeboard with a brief citation and the gift of a suitable memento.

I have also discovered sad examples of unrecognized excellence in quality endeavour. Once when visiting a factory I came across a supervisor in a remote laboratory on the site. He told me how his work group met regularly to progress their improvement activities and catalogued numerous successful projects that they had completed over a period of three years or more; his meetings had been religiously minuted and gave evidence of a little centre of excellence. Yet his efforts were completely unrecognized and indeed unknown by the site management. There was no culture existing that encouraged recognition of any sort, let alone peer group selection.

The principle of peer group selection must be carried into even the most formal recognition mechanisms organized on a corporate basis (see Chapter 4 and the 'hierarchy of acclaim'). When work groups select a recipient of the month – and it can be for quality, safety, environment, customer care or many other activities – the factory or office block or location then selects a quarterly recipient and finally there is a corporate annual award. The carrying through of the peer group selection principle is an essential element of success. In BP the company made a start down this road with the chairman's annual award for work in the safety field; it was a significant contribution to changing attitudes in the management of safety at all levels of the organization. It was also an important constituent of the corporate cement binding a very diverse organization together.

The assessment of those worthy of recognition can be facilitated by the use of tools and techniques. Peer groups in particular may need to be coached in these techniques, particularly in the use of self-assessment; these techniques are discussed in Chapter 10.

STARTING OUT

For those about to start out on the road of recognition – do not try to convert the world all at once. Be content to start small, select that area where you believe you have real influence, where a change in your style will have most impact. Yes! There is no escaping the truth that it is you who will have to change your behaviour first; and remember that you cannot introduce recognition in isolation – there are those other things like listening, coaching, trusting and involving too. Begin creating a new culture, light a small fire of change, start with 'casual' recognition, then recognize one or two special achievements or milestones and in doing this carefully judge the impact so that you can adjust your style until you get good acceptability and feed-back. When you know the appropriate tailoring for your group, you will able to apply all the options for recognition with confidence.

As we saw from the example of the TQ enthusiast manager earlier, when you have achieved some success, it may not go unnoticed. However, positively handled, it should be regarded as a germ of excellence that should be encouraged so that it may infect the wider organization. We must learn to utilize creative envy and the energy of discontent.

AVOIDING OVERSIGHT

In practising recognition you must be careful not to miss anyone out:

1. *On the margins.* It is all too easy to miss those in the far-flung outposts. In one case a very large and complex maintenance shut-down had been completed. The project had been completed on time and the plant was in production again on schedule. It was decided that this achievement should be recognized with a series of parties (shift workers were involved) for about 200 people in all. After the first of these, which had been very successful, a very angry call was received from someone who claimed to have been overlooked. He was the gatekeeper. He believed that he had made an important contribution to the effort in letting in the contractors, the lorries with materials, the cranes and so on. Whether or not his claim was a bit far-fetched, the point is that he wanted to be associated with the success and with the recognition of it.

2. *In the regions.* Another commonly overlooked group is the people who work in regional offices – sales offices are a good example. These are sometimes hundreds or even thousands of miles away from the source of the action. How easy it is to recognize a success in business without including them. Are they included in considerations for the 'hierarchy of acclaim'? Do they have their say in the selection of recipients? How do we make sure they receive their share of 'casual' recognition? Once, in my capacity as manager of quality implementation, I attended a meeting of regional sales managers, expecting to promote our latest thinking on culture change and continuous improvement, only to be met with a barrage of dissatisfaction caused by their perceived isolation and disconnection from the mainstream, so my agenda had to change from promotion to reclamation.

3 *The specialists.* Another group of people that we should be careful not to leave out in terms of recognition are those that we can call specialists. These may be specialists in some technical discipline where it may be difficult for the uninitiated to recognize worthy achievement. In such cases it is important for the right culture to exist to encourage their peers to recommend them for recognition. There are also those who are self-made specialists in an improvement technique by virtue of their own interest. For example, BP Chemicals trained over 500 people in statistical techniques in some depth. About 20 per cent of these became real enthusiasts and we designated them 'Champions' and facilitated the sharing of their developed skills with others. We also discovered many unsung heroes applying statistical techniques, sometimes self-taught, to great effect without the appropriate recognition.

CORPORATE AWARDS

In Chapter 4 the various national and international awards for corporate achievement in the field of total quality were set out as options. These awards are for excellence and they set high standards; they are not for the faint-hearted, the uncommitted or for those who have not an established TQ process of several years' standing. They all require absolute commitment from the top down and the allocation of significant resources. For example, a recent EQA winner had deployed a team of six people for many months exclusively to analyse and collate the inputs gathered from 28 000 employees in 15 countries, in order to prepare the written submission in their campaign to win the award. But more than this, they require every single employee to commit to the goal and to give a great deal extra of themselves to achieve it. On the plus side it is a massive positive learning experience. Many of the awards are similar in concept. They all include categories on leadership, quality planning, people development and management and customer satisfaction. Some have sections on QA and control, some have sections on process management, and a minority look at operational results as well as quality results. I will look at two of the best-known award schemes for TQM, and BS 5750/ISO 9000 for QA by way of examples.

The Malcolm Baldridge National Quality Award (MBNQA)

The Malcolm Baldridge National Quality Award (MBNQA, 1992), sponsored by the US federal government, assesses performance against the categories shown in Table 5.1.

TABLE 5.1   Performance categories of the MBNQA

	POTENTIAL POINTS
Leadership	90
Information and analysis	80
Strategic quality planning	60
Human resource development and management	150
Management of process quality	140
Quality and operational results	180
Customer focus and satisfaction	300
Total	1000

The European Quality Award (EQA)

The European Foundation for Quality Management (EFQM) was set up by 14 major European companies in 1988 with a declared aim of enhancing the position of European business in world markets through the medium of TQ (EFQM, 1994a). Its award borrows many of the features of the MBNQA but puts more emphasis on results splitting its categories into enablers (50 per cent) and results (50 per cent). It is usually most conveniently represented diagrammatically (Fig. 5.2).

Both the EQA and the MBNQA, and typically the other awards, require a written submission which is then examined by assessors and the best are selected for assessment visits. During these visits independent assessors prepare a report on the claims made in the submissions. The reports are then judged for the final awards.

● APPLICATION OF RECOGNITION IN PRACTICE

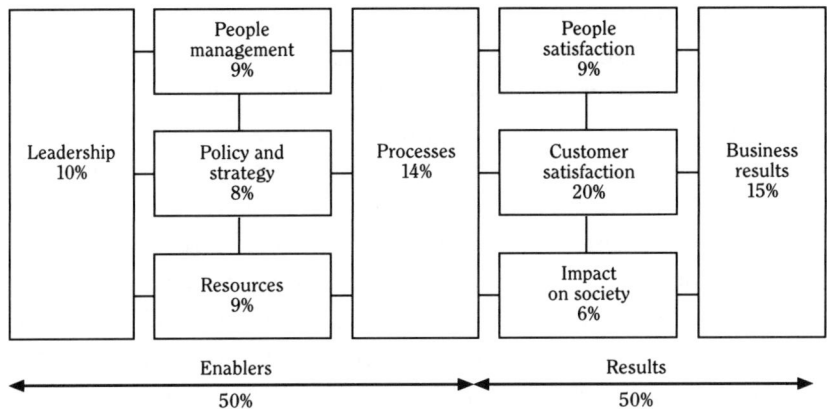

FIGURE 5.2   EFQM model
Source: EFQM

These assessment models are frequently used by organizations to monitor their own progress in total quality, whether or not they intend to make a submission for an award. For sure, some form of ongoing self-assessment is an essential prerequisite for any would-be applicant. There is further discussion of self-assessment in Chapter 10.

QA certification

BS 5750 (Parts 1, 2 and 3) and ISO 9001/2/3 were, to all intents and purposes, the same and the 1994 revision is now called BS EN ISO 9001, 2, 3. (BSI 1994).. Certificates indicating registration to the standards are awarded after independent third-party audit by accredited bodies. These bodies, often commercial auditing companies, are accredited by government sponsored organizations, e.g. the NACCB (National Accreditation Council for Certification Bodies) in the UK. Examples of some certification bodies are: BSI.QA, Lloyds Register QA, Det Norske Veritas, Bureau Veritas, ABS Quality Evaluations Inc., SGS Yarsley Quality Assured Firms, etc.

To achieve this recognition an appropriate management system must

MOTIVATING YOUR ORGANIZATION ●

be in place, understood and applied effectively by the employees, and properly documented. The first step is to design the system, then to write the required suite of controlled documentation which will include a quality manual, procedures and working instructions. The necessary controls must be identified and the calibration regimes prescribed. Then training of all personnel must take place and be put on record together with a programme for refresher training. The system must then be made to work. A programme of internal audits has to be established with its consequent corrective action system. When all of this has been done and there is an experience of some months' operation, a certification audit by an accredited third party can be undertaken. After registration to the appropriate standard and certification there will be further appraisal visits by the auditor to assure compliance; initially these will be every three months, reducing to every six months.

The QA standards are in several parts and it is only necessary to register to those parts that are seen as key to your business. The parts include these requirements:

Part 3   Management responsibility
   Quality system
   Contract review
   Document control
   Control of customer-supplied product
   Product identification/traceability
   Inspection and testing
   Control of testing equipment
   Inspection and test status
   Control of non-conforming product
   Corrective action
   Handling storage and delivery
   Records
   Internal audit
   Training
   Statistical techniques

Part 2   All of Part 3 plus

Purchasing control
Process control
Servicing

Part 1 All of Parts 2 and 3 plus
Specification, design and new product development

QA systems are far better if operated as an integral part of the TQ process rather than as a parallel and separate exercise.

CONCLUDING REMARKS

People want and even need recognition, but the correct environment, style or culture has to be present for it to be effective. This correct culture can only be created if managers at all levels – and it will be hardest for middle managers – are prepared to take the lead and change their behaviour first. Recognition of teams or individuals means picking them out from the rest of their group, in other words, making a selection. If this is not to be a source of discontent, this selection must involve peer groups.

Like many other parts of culture change, this small but good value-adding part called recognition needs pathfinders with the courage and vision to knock down barriers and withstand criticism. It also needs flexibility to tailor the approach, whether it be in a 'muck and bullets' production scenario, a small personnel department with lots of routine administration tasks, or a high-powered research department stuffed with academic glitterati. There can be no one best approach but each of them can improve their progress towards their goals with the judicious employment of recognition.

Those organizations wanting to avail themselves of corporate recognition in its several forms must indeed have long-term commitment to their quality process, well-developed self-assessment systems and an all-pervading, obvious and sustainable quality culture.

CHAPTER 6

Suggestion schemes

No book on reward and recognition would be complete without some mention of suggestion schemes. Not only because they have been around for more than 100 years and represent some of the earliest attempts to motivate and involve employees that did not involve physical abuse or intimidation; but also because, as a system of reward and recognition, they are very much alive and kicking today. In the UK alone there are believed to be more than 500 active suggestion schemes. The UK Association of Suggestion Schemes has over 100 paid-up members that include blue-chip companies like British Airways, the BBC, British Telecom, Barclays Bank, GEC, Southern Water, Sun Alliance Insurance Group, etc. All claim significant savings, often running into millions. In fact it has been estimated that well over £100 m per year are saved by the schemes and that over £10 m are paid out in awards.

SUGGESTION SCHEMES vs TQM

Is there a fundamental conflict? At this point I suspect that the TQ purists are starting to get a little nervous because, in an ideal TQ world, suggestions for improvement are part of all employees' normal responsibilities, indeed they have a duty to improve everything they do all of the time, and therefore they should not want or expect special payment or recognition for these ideas. There are no reward-based suggestion schemes in some of the standard-bearers of TQ, the European manufacturing operations of Japanese companies; in them improvement suggestions are very definitely part of the expected responsibilities of all workers and therefore not meriting any special reward or incentive. In fact several indigenous companies that have embarked on TQM have taken positive steps to terminate their suggestion schemes, often after many years of operation. Others have deliberately allowed them to atrophy by withdrawing active support. Yet others have successfully maintained their schemes in parallel with the TQ process.

The critics of the schemes will say that as well as inhibiting the free flow of ideas for improvement, these schemes can operate in the 'old' culture and do not require or promote culture change. This is true, but it does not have to be. It is possible to use an established suggestion scheme as a vehicle for cultural development and in this way to incorporate it within the TQ process. This is a view apparently shared by the EFQM as they include a question about suggestion schemes in their assessment questionnaire, 'People Management' (EFQM, 1994).

Example: value for money

A factory was in the throes of introducing TQM and the site steering committee came to debate the issue of the long-established suggestion scheme. It was on the agenda because on telling the employees that they were to be involved in the TQ process and their ideas used for improvement, many of them had said that they were glad to do this but that they would submit the ideas through the suggestion scheme in the hope of reward and recognition. So, inevitably there were those on the committee who argued that this was a barrier to the true TQ process and that the scheme should be terminated. There were also those managers who had found the scheme to be an irritant because it forced things on to their agenda that were not of their choosing, so they were in favour of termination for that wrong reason. At this point the chairman, the factory manager, asked how much the scheme had saved in the last three years: it was well over a million pounds! Could he be assured that the same level of saving would be achieved by TQM without the scheme? Only the most dedicated TQ converts were prepared to assert this; and so the site suggestion scheme was preserved. This coexistence produced some interesting results.

First, the administration of the scheme was sharpened up – how could it be said that people's ideas were needed if it took over a year to respond to them?! Second, in giving the scheme a new lease of life a climate of ideas generation was created and some ideas began to be brought out directly in work groups rather than through the scheme. Third, it was demonstrated to managers that if they were to respond promptly to suggestions and the suggestions were to be relevant to the strategic goals of the work group, then the members of the work group had better have a clear understanding of what those goals were. By giving them some direction, much of the trivial 'wish list' items were eliminated.

Individuals and teams

One argument is that suggestion schemes are designed to recognize individuals rather than teams, hence this encourages individualism, personal agendas and lower quality ideas. If this is true it takes but a simple change to the scheme rules to correct it. There is no reason at all why teams should not make suggestions and be empowered to decide among themselves how to divide the award.

Root-cause prevention

Some say that suggestion schemes produce fixes rather than root-cause preventive solutions. I think this is to underestimate employees; certainly with a little coaching in the principles of TQM and some good practical examples they will produce genuinely preventive suggestions.

Synergies with TQM

Opportunities for improvement
Rather than the apparent conflicts with TQM I would prefer to concentrate on the synergies. Most obviously, it seems to me that here we have an established means of identifying opportunities for improvement – key to the TQ process. It also embodies that other essential, namely measurement. Almost all schemes relate in some way the size of the award to the amount of saving likely to be achieved and that requires there to be measurement of the existing situation and the improvement. Above all, suggestion schemes are a first step to the participation and involvement that are essential ingredients of that most self-sustaining feature – ownership.

Plan-do-check-act
If an employee has proposed an improvement, he or she is going to be at the least interested in the implementation of that improvement. And here I believe there is a genuine criticism of schemes in the past which tended to separate the proposal of the idea from its implementation, often by a complex bureaucracy, managerial structures and/or departmental boundaries. Full ownership demands that the employee is involved at all stages of the Deming cycle (Deming, 1982).

Employers and employees
Suggestion schemes can be regarded in two ways. First from the employers' perspective: they are looking for higher productivity and opportunities for improvement. Then from the employees' point of view. They are looking for opportunities for recognition and, indeed, reward, but also for a conduit for upward communication. Whether we like it or not it was these schemes that provided one of the only ways that employees could communicate with their bosses in the cultures of the past 10 decades. The other way they had to invent for themselves, and that was the trade union, but its agenda was defensive, to minimize exploitation, which led to restrictive practices and similar negative cultural effects. To this day trade unions and employers

have difficulty trying to break out of their entrenched roles. So suggestion schemes had and still have the almost unique potential to weld together the aspirations of employers and employees within a joint ownership. This seems to be a good base from which to launch into a quest for a quality culture.

CASE STUDY

A survey conducted within BP Chemicals (S. Mahadevan 1992) revealed a rich variety of approaches as schemes had been developed locally and had been influenced by local cultures, management styles and attitudes.

The most formal scheme of all had an established structure and a printed booklet issued to all staff. It had a formalized eight-stage structured process of application, registration, filtering, technical evaluation, cost evaluation, decision, feedback and award. Over a two-year period 160 suggestions were received and nearly £30 000 was paid out in awards. Awards were presented by a senior manager at formal ceremonies with certificates given as well as cheques. These awards ranged from £5 for a well-meant, serious but impractical suggestion to a maximum of £2000. The majority were between £20 and £150 with 10 being in excess of £1000. The size of the award was judged on the basis of its originality, innovation and potential cost saving. Over 40 per cent of suggestions were implemented and saved an estimated £1.5 m per year in costs.

Much less formal schemes operated in some of BP's French locations. One, called 'Bourse aux Idées', had no formal procedure and relied entirely on the line management structure for appraisal and approval, a four-stage process which took less than a week to complete. As in the previous example the size of the award was decided by a 'diagonal slice' committee and was in the range 1000F to 10 000F.

At another small French location a simple suggestion scheme was limited to safety and security matters but yielded 200 submissions a year, of which 50 per cent received awards. Eighty per cent of these were implemented. Typically awards were in the region 300F to 1200F. General improvements were handled through a corrective action procedure introduced as part of the TQ process. So here was a stark example of the apparent dilemma of involving people in, and recognizing them for, improvement. The distinction between safety and general improvements is clearly historical and artificial.

Many quality systems within the company sought to introduce formal corrective action procedures that were more or less similar to those used in suggestion schemes. They differed crucially in that their purpose was not to motivate people by reward and recognition to become involved, but rather to bypass perceived management barriers to implementation. Experience of them is generally poor in that they fail because they are in fact seen to bypass the management line (increasing the isolation of middle managers) and are usually heavily bureaucratic. The best I have seen has been used to good effect at a factory that had no history of suggestion schemes: it was a simple five-stage process called a 'snag sheet' and as its name suggests was focused on those myriad of small improvements that we can all make in what we do – the principle of what the Japanese call *kaizen*:

$$1000 \times 0.001\% = 1\%$$

The most complex scheme that was discovered in the survey had 12 stages and perhaps not surprisingly was being allowed to atrophy by a studied lack of commitment and support.

THREATS AND OPPORTUNITIES

1 *Bureaucracy*. The last example above reflects a common opinion from those who are active subscribers to schemes that suffer from being over-bureaucratic. This, together with the apparent possible conflict with the principles of TQM can constitute a threat.
2 *Savings*. We have seen the size of the potential cost savings, which are confirmed by examples from other companies. British Rail estimates their saving to be over £5 m per year, British Airways over £2 m, ICI have quoted over £3 m, and stories of single suggestions yielding savings in six and seven figures are legion.

3 *Motivation and involvement.* In the UK the Industrial Society, a respected organization that promotes the greater involvement of all employees in the success of their enterprises, believes that suggestion schemes are a powerful method of motivating and involving employees and are also 'incredibly efficient' at increasing productivity and cutting costs.

SUGGESTION SCHEMES WITHIN TQM

In considering suggestion schemes within a TQ environment we must find a way to capture the benefits we have seen: to incorporate them, not abandon them. What is more I firmly believe that it can be done. The 1992 winners of the European Quality Award, Rank Xerox, describe in their written submission how they introduced a scheme into their UK operation in 1960 and that schemes are now in place in 19 European locations (Rank Xerox, 1992); their Austrian scheme is saving £25 000 per year and the Dutch version over 1.3 m Guilders. Far from declining, the number of suggestions submitted is on the increase.

We have seen that suggestion schemes provide a win/win solution to the goals of employers and employees alike. They stimulate the discovery of opportunities for improvement (the life-blood of any continuous improvement process). They create a platform for involvement and participation and they use reward and recognition to motivate. So we are a long way down the road to synergy with TQM.

We must now try to reduce the bureaucracy and hand the schemes back to the working line structures, working groups; empower them to administer the schemes within consistent guidelines; coach everybody to apply their innovative thoughts to customer satisfaction and the strategic goals of the group, business or factory; encourage process thinking by asking work groups to look at each part of their processes to build in improvement at each stage, and to measure their progress. Finally, we must carry the involvement that we have achieved through to the implementation stage of new ideas; we must bridge the disconnect that often exists. This can be done by teamwork, multi-discipline teams and cross-departmental teams.

My experience is that these applications will always enhance the solutions.

One example comes to mind: a small but involved job to modify a control loop on an effluent treatment system had been languishing on the backlog list for over a year since it had come in from the suggestion scheme, because it could not command priority in all of the departments concerned at the same time. The local work group were empowered to put together a team of operators (including the originator), instrument technicians, fitters and supervisors, and within 48 hours the system was installed and working.

Applying these changes to our approach we can plug in the energy of suggestion schemes to the Deming cycle of Plan–do–check–act, and we will have harnessed the potential of suggestion schemes to the power of TQM. This is a culture change, and again, by its nature, requires a change in behaviour. Difficult as this is, enlightened companies are doing so to good effect. Even exemplars of the quality method such as Nissan Motor Manufacturing (UK) Ltd have an Improvements Proposal Scheme (CHIPS) by which anyone can propose an improvement that is too large for their own work group to handle. Consistent with the Nissan style there are no awards or prizes, though one suggestion for a modification to an engine design that saved the Company £2 m did cause the management some heart-searching, and eventually they settled for the presentation of commemorative plaques by the managing director.

The Future

The company General Electric in the US has introduced a scheme called 'Work-Out' in which a series of local town hall-style meetings are held and employees invited to give their ideas for improvement. Management respond on the spot and publicly to the ideas that are raised and agree to implement about 90 per cent of them. There is also recognition for the initiator not only by publicity but also by awards such as stock options, cash ($100–200), dinner for two and so on. This is an example of a totally informal scheme that incorporates all the positive features of a scheme within a TQ type of environment: it has involvement, active listening, focus on the key processes of the business, rapid response, and recognition.

As shown by this example the trend will be towards incorporation within the TQM thinking. To achieve this the schemes will become less formal, they will be tailored to local requirements, evaluation will be decentralized, perhaps even down to team level, and cash awards will move downwards to emphasize recognition rather than beneficial income. The emphasis will move away from productivity towards motivation, creativity, involvement and recognition – to help reveal and reverse the 'hidden assumption' (see Chapter 3).

SUMMARY

1 Background
- Early attempts to motivate employees.
- Hundreds of companies, including blue chips, still use suggestion schemes.
- Savings in UK estimated at £100 m/annum.

2 Suggestion schemes and TQM
- Conflicting cultural messages.
- Schemes are vehicles for developing TQ culture.
- They are good value for money.
- They involve individuals and teams.
- They are readily modified to promote root cause prevention.

3 Synergies with TQM
- Opportunities for improvement.
- Promotes the Deming cycle.
- Communication/feedback channel between employees and employers.
- Mutually beneficial.

4 Examples
- Formal scheme yields regular savings.
- Two French schemes show it can be done with reduced bureaucracy,
- Corrective action schemes introduced in parallel are not a success.
- The most complex 12-stage scheme is dying out.

5 Threats and opportunities

- Threats are bureaucracy and conflict with TQM.
- Opportunities for savings, productivity, involvement and motivation.

6 Suggestion schemes in TQM
- Have these features:
  - incorporate rather than abandon
  - satisfaction for employees and employers
  - opportunities for improvement
  - involvement and participation
  - reward and recognition
- Do this:
  - hand back to work groups
  - empower them to administer
  - get involvement at all stages of the PDCA cycle.

7 Future
- Incorporate within TQM.
- Less formality – less bureaucracy.
- Recognition rather than beneficial income.
- Move from productivity to motivation, involvement, creativity and recognition.

CHAPTER 7

Options for reward

REWARD, PAY AND VALUE

Expressing concern about the use of jargon in management to disguise underlying trends, Susan Corby, who lectures in industrial relations at Manchester Metropolitan University, says that the use of reward rather than pay denotes some sort of prize dispensed by management (Corby, 1994). I disagree with this view. Reward is used to embrace everything that is received in return for work – all the benefits, including pay, which of course is the largest and most significant.

'We would work for nothing if we could afford to!' – the statement of well-motivated and stimulated professionals who show good employee satisfaction. Yes, perhaps, but the point is that they cannot afford to – pay is indeed necessary, if not a necessary evil (see Chapter 2). A recent survey (*Chemical Engineer*, 1993) in my own profession of chemical engineering showed that salary was fifth in a list of ten factors contributing to personal job satisfaction and there were many respondents who put it higher with these sort of comments: 'I need a good salary and time to spend with my family.' 'It's not worth working if you don't have time and money to do what you want after work.'

We have noted before that since pay is necessary we need to secure the best value from it: how can we get most motivation for our pounds or dollars?

PAY AS A MOTIVATOR

I am not going to revisit these arguments again, but simply restate the basics of my position:
- the voice of the people seems to suggest that pay is a motivator
- it sets the environment in which an employee's contribution is assessed
- if it is wrong, it will demotivate
- if it is wrong, no other motivation will work
- there are ways to create motivation from a reward system
- rewards and incentives must reflect the changes in culture that an organization is embracing; they must be aligned with the principles of TQM.

TARGETS FOR REWARD

In the first chapter of this book I talked about what makes people want to work – their motivation. It is interesting to develop this idea because we do not just want them to work but to work for *us*, rather than someone down the road. And not just to work for us rather than someone else, but to work well; and, because we espouse a total quality culture, to continuously improve their work. We want them to make a contribution, whether as organizers, administrators, doers, creative thinkers or innovators and to register achievement in one or more of these areas. But this is still not enough. If the work is to have some meaning it must be towards some end, a particular goal or target. That target has to be credible in terms of acceptable values and ethical standards as well as business success.

The reason that the world of work can be so richly satisfying is that it provides such a range of potential goals and targets for everyone, both collectively and individually. As we have seen before, these goals and targets must be transparently linked to strategic and business objectives but, more than that, there must be an obvious relationship with the reward policy too. An embarrassing question asked of one operating site was 'Why is it that your site is claiming the best performance in the company in terms of the appraisal of your employees, when you are not meeting any of the site objectives?' If credibility is to be sustained the reward system must have some linkage to results. In this context results do not only mean financial results but also customer satisfaction, safety and environmental performance and employee satisfaction. In a TQM situation it is important to include improvement targets in each of these areas (see Chapter 10).

BASIC PAY

Basic pay is the rate for the job and signifies the relative value of the job with respect to others within the organization and to the external local market. It does not reflect any unique skills or the achievement of an individual or any targets or goals. It assumes that all the incumbents of a particular job are of equal worth. This is a principle that is vigorously defended by trade unions for most craft and 'non-staff' jobs. It is a pillar of the solidarity that is the unions' power base, from which they exert their influence.

Time and overtime

In many cases basic pay refers to the time period of say 38 or 40 hours per week with the implication that any time worked over and above this will attract additional payments usually at enhanced rates, i.e. overtime pay. This principle becomes more diffuse as one moves into the 'staff' jobs and to all intents and purposes disappears with progress up the scale of seniority. Overtime pay is sometimes grouped by some into a category called 'sacrifice pay' along with other allowances such as shift allowances, abnormal working allowances, etc. It indicates that these payments are to compensate for intrusions into people's free time. However, as patterns of work change, less and less people work standard hours and more of those who are in work, work longer hours. Thus it will be seen as less of an abnormality, less of a sacrifice and will attract less exceptional pay.

Cost of living

For a long time cost-of-living payments were the only form of improvement that could be expected and became virtually automatic; some pay formulae were in fact linked to the cost-of-living index. Not only is this inflationary at the macro-economic level and uncompetitive at the company level but it has no motivational value at all.

Motivation

If it is to set an environment in which employees are going to feel comfortable in their work, basic pay must be in line with the going rate for the job and be felt fair in relative terms to other jobs. Beyond that it is the prospect of improvement to rates of pay or to earning potential that is motivating.

BASIC PAY PLUS INCOME IMPROVERS

Basic pay is thus a minimum reward, it has no motivational impact and all recipients will naturally be seeking to augment it. There is an inherent drive to differentiate one's individual contribution in some way, whatever the trade union may say. What is more, there is an expectation that the means of augmentation will be available. So, over the years, ways of enhancing basic pay have evolved to include elements of recognition within the reward system to motivate and to encourage identification and ownership within the enterprise.

Performance-related elements

The direct linkage of part of the pay package to performance is an attractive idea in terms of motivation. It is also a powerful instrument to reinforce the direction of cultural change in that those who exhibit the desired behaviour and achieve in the right direction can be seen to benefit through their rewards. For these reasons more and more organizations are adopting this format and applying it across a wider and wider spectrum of employees. The proportion of the pay package that is variable in this way is typically up to 12 or 15 per cent.

The whole subject of performance-related pay (PRP) usually generates an emotional response as well as a raft of very reasonable questions. We all have a natural reticence to submitting to scrutiny by others and immediately call into question the judgement or methods of measurement. Extreme examples of this were seen recently in the UK by the reaction of teachers to a suggestion for PRP and by the police in their reaction to the Sheehey Report (1993), one of the recommendations of which was for PRP. (Chapter 8 discuses this subject in more detail.)

Skill-based payments

Skill-based payments have been around a long time. These recognize those employees with required skills and in particular those who are multi-skilled. An employee with additional skills over and above those evaluated for the basic pay, and especially those with a sufficient range of skills to do any job in a particular unit, cell or team can add significant value through that flexibility. Additional payments are made for the acquisition of these skills.

Multi-skilling, or the learning of more than one skill by each employee, is a necessary consequence of job enrichment to the 'whole job' system. The more enlightened trade unions see that this is an inevitable development for the future and seek to secure the appropriate rewards. Some unions representing the traditional crafts in the UK have mounted a rearguard action in an attempt to defend the exclusivity of their turf, and to dissuade their members from trespassing on others' turf. There will always be areas of exclusive turf: skills that are too specialized, too arduous to learn or too infrequently required to make it worthwhile training multi-skilled workers in them.

The problem with skill-based pay is that it rewards the acquisition of useful skills as an end in itself, without reference to their application to the job in hand or to the improvement process. As such it is not only expensive, but lacks any focused motivation. Much better to reward the improvement resulting from the application of those skills and to create a demand for training from the needs of the improvement process. Demand-driven training of this sort is certain to add value, not cost.

Service payments

This is a form of basic pay improvement that is commonly employed. Each year of service is rewarded by a basic pay enhancement up to some maximum achieved in, say, five years. It is a reward for continuing to belong to an organization. This has little motivational impact and may not even encourage loyalty, but it does contribute to the employment environment and helps to increase the comfort factor. In practice it means that there is not a rate for the job but rather a band or scale of pay for each job.

This system was a characteristic of the larger Japanese firms where a policy of pay-by-age was in place for years; it was linked to the employment-for-life ethic. This system gave a guarantee of earnings progression up to a peak in the forties age range after which there would be a gradual decline.

BASIC PAY PLUS RESULTS-BASED INCREMENTS

Bonuses

Bonuses are lump sums typically paid annually and linked directly to performance. The performance recognized is sometimes related to specific elements of the work and sometimes reflects the overall contribution. Some companies pay senior staff bonuses in kind rather than cash, in gold, diamonds or even coffee and wine. These are attempts to avoid tax both to the company and the individual, and as the authorities legislate against each of these loopholes, so the ingenious tax avoider discovers a new one – the latest is in redeemable life insurance policies.

Bonuses are also paid by-the-event; this is in effect direct cash recognition but may be none the worse for that provided that it does not conflict with non-cash recognition schemes and is acceptable to the majority of non-recipients according to the local culture. The more immediate a cash award the greater will be the effect in terms of recognition.

The award of bonuses, whether we like it or not, is a powerful signalling mechanism. Therein lies a danger because it is very easy to send the wrong signals by looking only at the merits of individual cases without the cultural context. By way of example, in the chemical industry it used to be common practice to recognize and reward by bonuses those who contributed to the recovery of plants from crises like crash shut-downs or equipment failures or emergency situations – fine, but what about those whose plants did not shut down or fail, how was their performance recognized? In other words there was a dramatic endorsement of crisis management, and, surprise, surprise, that industry had the best crisis managers in the world! Recently this has been corrected using annual bonuses and performance-related pay.

Bonuses in kind to a selected few senior staff also give signals which have little to do with recognition, but perhaps say something about the giver.

At-risk elements

This is an extreme version of PRP in which part of the potentially available reward is absolutely dependent on the achievement of a target – no achievement, no pay. This can be refined to a scheme where the amount of reward depends on the amount by which a target is exceeded. Such schemes are often applied to the most senior echelons of management and can lead to dramatic, if not grotesque, increases in salary. Some examples of this have been senior executives of the newly privatized public utilities in the UK, though it is also common, if not so much in the public eye, in private industry and commerce. The method can cause an unacceptable range of differentiation across an organization.

The most extreme examples of at-risk pay are those that work on a commission only or self-employed basis. They certainly know about the motivating effects of pay. Employers of commission-only workers often use the numbers principle of percentage success. For example, if it is known that about ten per cent of initial sales contacts are successful, then the thing to do is increase the number of contacts by increasing the number of agents. This can result in a lamentable lowering of standards with the consequent effect on quality for the customer.

Profit sharing

This dates back to the turn of the century and has been employed to give a sense of purpose and belonging to employees. It is less certain that it contributes to motivation at the day-to-day working level. It is a mutual benefit which means that it is distributed universally among all personnel with no reference to individual performance. It depends for any success it may enjoy on there being some profits to share. The problem with schemes based crudely on corporate financial results is that there are many influences on those results that are perceived to be out of the control of individuals or groups of employees, and the gearing of those influences can be high.

Share schemes are a form of profit sharing that positively link the employee to the fortunes of the Company as measured from the shareholders' viewpoint. A criticism is that they elevate this viewpoint above those of the other stakeholders. Like simple profit sharing they do not differentiate individuals' or teams' contributions but assume that all employees should enjoy equal benefit. This is fair enough in that it is seen to be a broad brush, 'we are all in it together' type of identifying reward, but then some companies spoil this effect by offering even more favourable and highly lucrative share options to the most senior staff.

An option is the right to buy shares in the future at a price determined today. If the company is successful and share values increase there will be significant financial advantage. There is a positive incentive here to improve for those that are seen to have most influence on the financial success of the company. It is also an incentive that is linked to longer-term success, which is compatible with the desired culture. Once the option beneficiary is a significant shareholder he may well begin to be more concerned with the short-term shareholder's interests in performance. But it is the disparity within the hierarchy which is created that is the most damaging because it is based on the false premise that loyalty and consistency of effort can only be expected from the highest echelons. Share options for all employees have to be considered in genuine participative, involved cultures (an example is given in Chapter 9).

Peter Thompson, Chairman of the National Freight Corporation has written about introducing an employee share scheme to a new company (Thompson, 1990). He believes it had a real role to play in creating a sense of identification with the success (or failure) of the enterprise and catalysing a real culture change from time serving and wage taking to contributing and improvement seeking. However, he makes the point that it is necessary to keep share ownership and employment separate. Neither promotion or, if it comes to it, redundancy can be influenced by share ownership.

Participation in most share schemes is voluntary and therefore they have to be demonstrably generous to encourage a wide take-up.

There is one further benefit that organizations can draw from employee share ownership and that is that it provides a route to the appointment of employee directors by election. This is not the place to enter into the argument for or against such appointments except to say that the presence of employee directors must be a powerful signal about the culture of the company and a continuing influence on the direction of change.

The trade union position on profit sharing and share schemes is that the unions prefer the giving of cash 'up-front'. They are suspicious of share schemes, particularly if it gives individual employees a voice in the company's affairs. They believe that if anyone is to represent employees' interests on boards of directors, it should be a trade union nominee who can put the official collective policy and preserve their power base.

Gainsharing

Gainsharing is a technique to allow those who are being asked to improve their work to share in the benefits of that improvement; the earliest schemes were simply based on productivity. Productivity payments are designed to be counter-inflationary, to be self-funding, to increase pay without adding to costs. This, of course, is a sounder concept for basic pay improvement but only begins to have a motivational impact in the second year of application.

There have been some innovative schemes based on incentives for productivity; two examples both originated in the USA:
- The Rucker plan: A.W. Rucker called his plan a 'share of production

plan' and it thus had some features of the more sophisticated gainsharing schemes that were to follow (see below). He established a ratio of wages to added value and set a standard based on results over a period of six years. The proceeds of any improvement on that standard were placed in a fund, 40 per cent of which was paid back to employees in the form of bonuses. Three-quarters of the bonuses were paid monthly and the remainder was held until the end of the year.

- The Scanlon plan: developed by J.N. Scanlon, this was similar to the Rucker plan except that rather than added value in production it took the net sales value and all manpower costs, direct and indirect. The distribution of the proceeds was similar to Rucker's but in this case 60 per cent of the proceeds were returned to the employees.

Both of these schemes reward productivity on a site-wide basis and do not differentiate the contributions of individuals or smaller teams.

The crudest form of productivity incentive is to pay only for output produced. An example of this is 'piece work' where a worker will only get paid a rate per item produced. It has been applied in industries such as garment manufacturing and outwork in which materials are delivered to the workers' homes where they make them up or assemble them. It is often characterized by low piece rates, which expose the method to straying over the boundaries of exploitation if not accompanied by a strong package of intrinsic provisions (life-enhancing elements, working environment, etc.).

Another example is commission-only payments particularly applied to selling situations. Again this has the inherent danger of the sale being the overriding priority rather than customer satisfaction. There are some notorious examples of this in the financial services sector.

Payment by results is primarily designed to minimize unit costs and overheads, but clearly it does motivate people – no work, no pay! But it neither encourages managers to develop a TQ culture or the workers to consider anything other than volume output, and certainly not customer-focused improvement.

All schemes based on productivity have some compelling arithmetic associated with them:

Increased productivity = more work with the same people
OR = the same work with less people,
more work = more product,
more product = more sales
OR = increasing stocks
which = less work
= less people,
less people = redundancy

There are millions of people in the western economies that have become experts in these equations during the 1990s. So the impact of productivity as a motivational improvement to basic pay depends on the economic environment: boom means more for all, recession has meant downsizing, rationalization and redundancy. In this recessional case it is essential to be seen to work hard to minimize the impact of reduction by trying to differentiate market performance through customer satisfaction, and by treating those who have to go in the most sensitive and generous manner that can be devised. In fact, a real case for the ideas of TQM.

Gainsharing is enjoying a revival after the early efforts of many years ago. It is attractive to the TQ culture type because it focuses the reward system directly on improvement. The schemes depend on measured improvement against a pre-selected range of criteria. The key to gainsharing is that a proportion of the benefits of these improvements is committed to rewarding those responsible for the achievement.

These features have appeared in productivity incentive schemes like the Rucker and Scanlon plans mentioned above. The advantage of such schemes is that they are more independent of external forces and the participants are assured of sharing in the fruits of their efforts. It is one of the most culturally defensible systems to align with total quality management.

Edward Lawler (1992) points out that the increasing popularity of gainsharing, especially among larger organizations such as General Electric, Rockwell, 3M, Motorola, Monsanto, etc., is that they incorporate the reward system into the 'way of managing'. He also asserts that these systems cannot be expected to produce benefits unless they are part of a process of cultural change involving new behaviours throughout the organization.

Human resources academics Newstrom and Davis (1993) also say that gainsharing schemes use fundamental ideas from organizational behaviour; they encourage suggestions, teamwork and improved communications, and are dependent on there being a participative environment.

BASIC PAY PLUS STATUS SYMBOLS

Perquisites

'Perks are undesirable and should be phased out.' A rational statement to which most thinking people would subscribe, and yet perks persist and, indeed, seem resistant to all attempts to reduce them. The reason that they do not align well with TQM is that they are almost always used to mark status or position rather than performance or the display of essential behaviours. They are part of the culture that relied on the promise of promotion as a motivator. Many of them are financial in nature, such as access to share options, but the ultimate perk and still the most persistent is the company car. The anticipation of this benefit still feeds the ambition of many a young executive. The cult of the company car has developed over the years into its own sophisticated hierarchy, graduating from the Ford or Toyota to the BMW, Jaguar or Lexus, many schemes having several stages in between. At last these schemes seem to be in decline now because of the escalating costs of maintaining them and the reduction in the tax advantage as the revenue authorities have caught up.

Promotion

Promotion has always been an obvious way of advancing salary. Its motivating effect is more in the anticipation than the fact and lasts for a relatively short period after the event. As organizations become flatter and less hierarchical, other methods will have to be found to satisfy the natural expectation of all for income progression. The Japanese company Marumara developed a system of non-specific job titles to overcome this problem so that as well as their standard rank system of post titles such as department head, deputy head, etc., they had a parallel series of non-specific titles such as executive, counsellor and so on.

Privileges

Thirty or so years ago it was not uncommon for there to be as many as four different restaurants for employees to eat their daily meals, and which one you used depended only on status. The same was true of wash-rooms, car parks, first-class travel, which floor of the building one worked on and so on. In the 1990s not all of these quaint practices have been swept away; there may only be two restaurants now but how many senior managers have reserved parking? Certain privileges go with the achievement of a certain position and enhance the anticipation of promotion; a bigger office, a carpet on the floor, better furniture, a personal secretary, a reserved parking place, executive wash-rooms, executive dining-rooms, as well as the financial perks.

The problem with privileges of this sort is not their cost, but the message that they give: the relative value of the manager's job cannot be denoted by pay alone, it needs all these additional symbols! This is clearly not true, so the message that will be received is that there are two sorts of people employed in the organization, one of which is more worthy than the other. If this is true we should not be surprised if there are at least two sets of objectives and agendas.

These privileges are archaic and in general should be dispensed with in the cultures of the 1990s. If they exist at all, they should only be used as a means of short-term recognition (see Chapter 4).

BASIC PAY PLUS LONG-TERM BENEFITS

These are generally of the life-sustaining kind such as pension schemes, widows' benefits, life insurance, health insurance, child care and subsidized meals at work. They are for most people an extremely important part of the reward package. But they are less to do with motivation than with being part of the ethos of a decent employer. They create an atmosphere of care and value for individual employees. They are about recruitment and retention rather than improvement and achievement.

In the modern environment of no-job-for-life, outsourcing, contracting and organizations with only a small permanent nucleus of key employees, the provision of these types of benefit is likely to decline.

Differentials

The differentials between jobs are a feature of pay policy that has to be got right or it will certainly demotivate. There has to be some obvious rationale that is credible to the majority. So it seems difficult to argue against some form of formal 'job evaluation' based on assessment of skill development, responsibility, accountability, size of the operation, qualifications, training, impact on the company's reputation, etc.

The range of differentials across an organization also requires attention. This will vary with the size of the company and the financial responsibility of the most senior people. Whereas we might find it reasonable to justify a ten-fold difference bottom to top, it may be difficult to explain a fifty-fold difference. There may be an argument for very high differential ranges in high tax economies, in which case the differentials in after-tax pay becomes a useful metric.

The final comment on differentials is about the impact of flatter non-hierarchical organizations. As the traditional structures crumble, the status and salary equation becomes less absolute and we need to find new criteria for evaluation. Experience, job knowledge, specialist skills and behaviour development will all feature more strongly.

The culture change requires a commensurate change in the attitudes to pay. Members of teams may be working towards shared goals but will have to accept that they may have markedly different basic pay based on skills, qualifications and experience. Diagonal slices across the skills and experience spectrum will be common within teams.

SUMMARY
1 Pay is necessary so how can we get most value from our reward systems?
2 It is possible to organize payment policy to motivate employees to follow the cultural direction set in the strategy of an organization.
3 If the reward policy is not aligned with the improvement culture it will be a serious barrier.
4 Basic pay must be a platform for motivation.
5 Basic pay must promote a general feeling of comfort and fairness, in both absolute levels and differentials.
6 There must be a mechanism for income improvement.
   - Income improvers
     - performance-related elements
     - skill-based payments
     - service payments.
   - Results-based increments
     - bonuses, annual and by-the-event
     - at-risk elements
     - profit sharing
     - share schemes
     - gainsharing, productivity (e.g. some early schemes – Rucker and Scanlon); output pay; the arithmetic of productivity; a modern revival of gainsharing.
   - Status symbols
     - perks
     - promotion
     - privileges.
   - Long-term benefits
     - pensions
     - life insurance
     - health insurance
     - child care
     - subsidized meals.
7 The differential range across an organization must be considered and credible.

● OPTIONS FOR REWARD

The range of options available to the builder of a reward system (see Chapter 9) is summarized in Fig. 7.1.

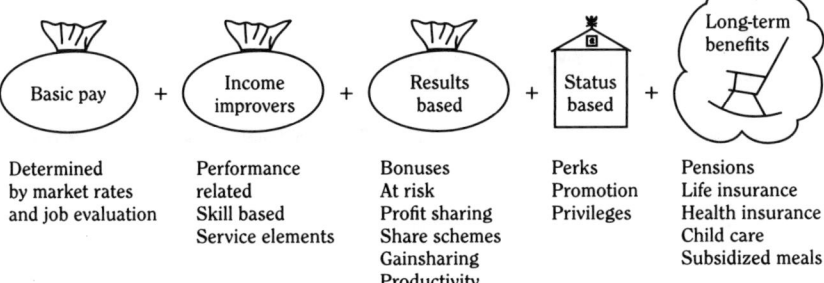

Basic pay	Income improvers	Results based	Status based	Long-term benefits
Determined by market rates and job evaluation	Performance related Skill based Service elements	Bonuses At risk Profit sharing Share schemes Gainsharing Productivity	Perks Promotion Privileges	Pensions Life insurance Health insurance Child care Subsidized meals

FIGURE 7.1 Options for reward

CHAPTER 8

Performance-related rewards

The idea of performance-related rewards has gained credence as we have entered an economic environment of low single-figure inflation. When cost of living rises were 20 per cent plus, it was not possible to consider performance awards that meant anything in comparison. This movement coincided with some cultural changes like the 'enterprise culture' and continuous improvement through total quality, both of which reinforce the thinking behind performance awards. The view of the Confederation of British Industry (the most influential employers' organization in the UK) is '... that financial incentives combined with good employee involvement and communication can lead to greater employee commitment to their company and a greater understanding of business realities' (CBI, 1980).

Academics and human resource professionals disagree about the effectiveness of performance relating and it has to be said that there is little hard research evidence to suggest that it actually has an effect on standards of performance. But for me it is the linkage with the culture of continuous improvement of performance that is vital. The instrument of pay is used to deliver positive strokes to recognize those that are successfully adapting to the desired culture. Dale and Cooper (1992), writing on TQ and human resources, state that there should be a direct clear and explicit link between performance, outcomes and rewards. Employees must experience the performance-outcome connection.

On the face of it the concept of linking the amount of pay received by employees to how well they do their jobs is simple. But because income is a measure of our value, if that income becomes variable and the variation is dependent on the judgement of others we become nervous and are prompted to ask some questions.

Who judges the performance?

Though this is often the first question, in industry and commerce it is not as contentious as may be imagined. After all, traditionally most income progression has been in the hands of the employers or their agents – managers and supervisors – and significantly influenced by them. The fact is that judgement will be made and will occasionally be flawed. To reduce the incidence of such problems many organizations have attempted to reduce the subjective element by the introduction of forms of measurement (see Chapter 10). These measurement systems are linked closely with formal appraisals which are usually carried out by immediate line managers.

Groups of workers represented by trade unions have often been excluded from performance-related pay usually as a result of the contention that fair unbiased judgements could not be made. I suspect that this assertion disguised the real reason for their opposition which was a perceived threat to solidarity. Other groups still resist PRP on the grounds that there can be no satisfactory judgement of performance; these include those in the service professions such as teachers, doctors, nurses and police.

Individuals or teams?

These days we increasingly emphasize that it is team performance that is important and most effective in improving results, yet we pay people as individuals. It is often argued that stressing the performance element of pay for individuals undermines teamwork. So which performance is going to be related to pay, the individual's or the team's? There are some supplementary questions as well:

1. *Should all team members receive the same reward for the same performance?* We all know those members of the team who have not measured up – must we accept that they receive equal reward? If the team is mixed-disciplined, diagonally sliced with a wide range of basic salaries, it is likely that there will be a range of values to the contributions of individual members.
2. *What about multiple teams?* Many people will be members of more than one team – does that make team reward impossible?
3. *Can individual performance be rewarded?* An individual may have turned in an exceptional performance – can he or she be rewarded individually without threatening the harmony of the team?

Until now, individual reward has predominated and has the clear advantage of imparting a sense of self-worth which we should take care to protect. Most of the questions above are answered by the pervading attitudes of the culture that exists in the workplace and as that culture changes so will the answers. We have to be sure that the reward policies are always aligned, in step with, if not leading and encouraging, the changes.

WHAT PERFORMANCE?

There are many potential answers to this question too.

1. *The overall performance of the company.* Certainly this gives a sense of belonging, of being involved in the enterprise, but the larger that enterprise is the more difficult it is for an individual to engage directly with the result.
2. *The performance of a business stream.* Within companies there are often specific business streams or product lines with which groups of employees can identify. The results of these businesses will often mean much more to employees in terms of their personal involvement.
3. *The performance of a site, office or location.* This is often an appropriate metric with which many employees find it easy to identify.
4. *The performance of a team.* This gives clear recognition of the

contribution towards a shared objective as well as enhancing the team culture.
5 *Performance against individual goals and objectives*. This is often the simplest to understand. It can be a powerful motivator but can be hard to devise quantitative measures.

How can performance be defined and measured?

If this question can be adequately answered, then most of the other questions are resolved or assume less importance. An adequate answer is one that does not fall foul of the criticisms of inconsistency and consequent divisiveness.

It is the inability to provide satisfactory answers in the public services that is a major barrier in that sector. How do you measure the performance of a nurse or a policeman? However, all activities can be measured if we are ingenious enough to devise the means; but some of the 'softer' issues such as behaviour can be more subjective. The area of measurement is key to the whole subject of performance-related pay, and indeed to the practice of reward and recognition, and will be discussed in detail in Chapter 10.

Is it fair?

There has always been comparison of pay, one with another, although on an individual basis there has always been an attempt to preserve confidentiality. Pay scales have been public knowledge but position on the scale has not. When a further degree of variation through performance is introduced, the possibility of comparisons leading to claims of unfairness is increased. Any scheme that assumes and relies on secrecy will fail. PRP systems must be as transparent as possible and their robustness to criticisms of unfairness will depend entirely on the definition and measurement of the performance (see above and Chapter 10).

Is the reward committed or results dependent?

Performance-related pay has to be paid for, and if a company is not performing well, it will be inclined to reduce or abandon PRP. In the case in which PRP is linked only to corporate performance the reaction is automatic, but in other cases there can be problems. If a business, site, or team has surpassed all of its objectives and is then told that the corporate results are poor and therefore there is little or no money for PRP, then the motivational effects will be destroyed for at least a year. Perhaps worse still, the culture of improvement, involvement and empowerment will be seen to be misaligned. So we have to invent ways of making a commitment to PRP. Employees must be confident that if they achieve a good performance then their pay will indeed reflect that achievement. Some of these ways are discussed in Chapter 9 – they involve the use of benefits generated by the improved performance.

Who allocates PRP?

Assuming resources have been found to fund PRP, who decides on the allocation? Pay policy is naturally seen as part of the personnel (or HR) function. So the corporate personnel department will work out an allocation formula that is designed to be fair to all. These formulae are often so complex that no one really understands them, much less can they communicate the rationale behind any particular individual reward. To overcome this, some companies delegate the allocation to local managers, giving them a purse of money to award as they see fit. In the ultimate, allocation is delegated down to team level, where team leaders disperse the available funds. In the most open, empowered cultures, the team may decide within itself who gets what.

In my experience it is easier to delegate the dispersion of funds for performance bonuses than for performance elements of pay. The latter do require greater guidance and conformity if they are to be felt fair.

What will it cost?

There are two elements to the cost. One is the cost of the actual award and the other is the management cost of administering the schemes. The award costs will either be met from the salaries and wages budget, in which case it is a matter of allocating the available funds between basic pay and PRP, or they will be met from the accrued benefits of improvements as in gainsharing and productivity schemes. The differential administrative costs are in the management time needed to set targets, assess performance, communicate with teams and individuals, and allocate funds. All of these activities are necessary anyway and are part of what Philip Crosby (1979) called the Cost of Quality:

Cost of Quality = Price of Conformance + Price of Non-conformance

They are part of the Price of Conformance and, Crosby argued, will be more than countered by the reduction in the Price of Non-conformance.

PRP and TQM

Performance-related pay existed before total quality management and can and does exist outside it, but there are special considerations where there is an attempt to establish TQM. This is because TQM asserts that customers are key and if they are to be satisfied there has to be a regime of continuous improvement. If that is to succeed all employees must be involved and understand that they each must continuously improve what they do.

Link reward to TQM

Recognition is an established part of the culture that supports these efforts. In the same way reward must be linked in too. The reward systems cannot be in any way opposed to this culture or even in parallel with it but rather must be an integral part of it. It is fatal to be seen to be recognizing some performance that does not conform to the thrust of TQ. PRP is a strong lever and must be deployed to support the TQ culture, to recognize achievements and behaviour that spring from a good understanding of its principles and practice.

Teams, TQM and reward

Teams and teamwork are effective mechanisms for the application of continuous improvement and any PRP system must reinforce this practice by being set up to recognize performance within teams. Teams should not be formed and their performance judged without there being a thought-through system of reward to hand.

TQ and the dangers of PRP

TQ comes to the aid of PRP by counteracting one of its greatest dangers. When people understand that part of their income is dependent on performance they will apply Pitts's Law. This law states that if a system or policy is exploitable it will be exploited. So there will be those who direct all their energies to demonstrating personal achievements. It is their income at stake so they will have scant consideration for their team, much less the business or company. Excellence for them will be defined by the size of their PRP. Energy will be diverted to a series of private strategies. What is more, in the most extreme cases there will be little regard for how these private goals are achieved – the ends (PRP) justify the means. Traditional pay is reviewed annually and any PRP is adjudged annually too. Therefore any achievement must be demonstrated within this one-year time span – what an incentive for short-termism, the very antithesis of TQM!

These dangers are not restricted to any particular level in the organization; in fact, at-risk pay, which is commonest at the senior levels, has the most extreme incentive for this behaviour. When it comes into play at these senior levels it can influence and modify the strategies of a company and threaten its declared values.

Another danger is that PRP encourages the high achievers but penalizes the non-achievers and can drive them into a spiral of despair as the differentials widen. TQ again comes to the rescue because it focuses on improvement and asserts that any performance, however poor, can be improved. So, if improvement targets are set rather than absolute ones this danger can be reduced and eliminated.

All of this paints PRP in a pretty black light. In fact much of the bad press that PRP has attracted is due to attempts to impose it without the benefit of the appropriate cultural background (see Chapter 12). The introduction of PRP in the absence of the correct environment will improve nothing. It is by the application of the principles of TQ as an overriding consideration for the assessment of performance that solutions can be found, and the motivating effects of PRP can be released with minimum danger.

SOLUTIONS

Because TQ focuses all activities on the customers' requirements, to be done right first time, every time and calls for certain behaviour patterns to allow that to happen, thus it constrains the worst excesses of blind self-interest. TQ represents the belief that by concentrating on the way that we do everything we do and trying to improve it we will achieve the desired results. This is a cogent counter to the short-term, here today gone tomorrow operator. It is not just what we achieve, but how we achieve it that in the long term will provide sustainable performance. It is this that should be recognized through PRP.

- What and how: it is comparatively easy, and therefore very common, to reward results, the attainment of an objective. But if we try to balance that achievement with an element of reward based on the methods used and the style of its achievement there will be an immediate change in perceptions.
- Skills: part of the 'how' will be the beneficial application of developed skills. There are so many skills and techniques available to help in the improvement of all facets of work, and companies allocate a great deal of human resources and large sums of money to training their employees in these skills. But how many of them either measure the benefit to their key processes of all that training or reward successful application to real work situations?
- Behaviour: as a vital constituent of culture change it seems entirely reasonable that we should reward those who demonstrate those behaviours that we believe to be essential to the successful progress

of change. In fact, I would say that it is essential that we are seen to be rewarding these behaviours, because at the outset, there will be only a few pathfinders who have sufficient confidence and courage to change behaviour from the established norm. They will have to suffer the suspicion and even ridicule of their colleagues before these new behaviours can be established. Equally it is essential that we do not reward those who exhibit blatantly counter-cultural behaviour – the ends must not justify any means.

- Radicals for change: we must encourage and motivate by reward those among our people who are prepared to risk something, whether it be their status, their reputation or even their PRP to catalyse change. These may be difficult people to manage in the conventional sense, but we need them, the lateral and upside-down thinkers. And we need them in positions of influence. There is a tendency to identify these characters and to move them into a specialist, advisory or coordinating role; this is often to marginalize them and expose them as eccentrics. No, we have to have the boldness to leave them, or place them in line roles where they can act as exemplars for all and accelerate the pace of change.
- Local relevance: in terms of the publicity for change, the sending of signals, it is important that rewarded performance has immediate credibility at local level. The achievements against targets, in improvement in behavioural change and skill deployment, must be relevant to the local aspirations and cultural thrust. Like the TQ process itself, it must be tailored to the local requirements of the organization and grow out of its traditions. Just as there is no such thing as *the* total quality process, so there is no such thing as *the* PRP system. In very large and diverse organizations, the implication of this is that PRP that is only linked to corporate performance will have little impact.
- Simple measures: complex formulae for determining PRP are to be avoided – they are the breeding grounds for misunderstanding and discontent. Measurement defines performance, therefore it is important that it is simple and well understood by the whole population. It is also a subject area that generates a good deal of emotion because it is through measurement that we express the value of individual and team

contributions and, perhaps even more sensitive, the means by which we compare them one with another. For all of these reasons measurements must be developed in a participative way and they must enjoy wide ownership by those to whom they will be applied. The subject of performance measures is discussed in more detail in Chapter 10.
- Teams and individuals: the use of teamworking to achieve continuous improvement may suggest that individual performance reward is dead. This is a misconception because there is no reason why the individual's performance within a team should not be recognized and rewarded. Indeed there is every reason why it should be strongly encouraged because it is in this context that there is a counter to the private agenda. Although performance within and of teams will become more and more dominant, there will always be individual performance worthy of reward and recognition.

Summary

1 Income is seen as a measure of personal value. Subjective variations to income, such as performance-related pay, prompt questions:
   - Who judges the performance?
   - Performance of individuals or teams?
   - What performance? The company, the business, the site, the team?
   - How is performance defined and measured? All activities can be measured but 'soft' issues are more subjective.
   - Is the reward committed or results dependent? The impact of external factors on qualifying performance can be demotivating.
   - Who allocates PRP? Delegate as close to the workplace as possible.
2 Total quality management comfortably embraces PRP because it is a powerful way of using pay policy to recognize performance and such recognition is an established part of a TQ culture.
3 Such an effective lever as PRP must not be deployed in any way not aligned to the culture change philosophy. PRP on its own improves nothing.
4 There are dangers of private agendas and short-termism in PRP, but TQM is effective in controlling these dangers.

5 Thus the difficulties of PRP can be solved by:
   - balancing the results with how they were achieved
   - rewarding the beneficial application of developed skills
   - rewarding those who demonstrate the essential behaviours for a TQ culture
   - rewarding and placing in positions of influence those who are prepared to risk being radicals for change
   - giving local relevance to rewarded performance
   - using simply understood and accepted measures of performance
   - being prepared to reward both team and individual achievement and the contribution of individuals within a team.
6 There are nearly as many arguments against performance-related pay as for it, but when it is positioned within TQ it can be a forceful recognition of improvement and a foundation part of the supporting structure of the culture.

Application of reward in practice

A reward is a compound of basic pay with improvement mechanisms and performance-related elements. To align a reward system to the TQ culture we must put together a practical working scheme that has these characteristics:
- open and transparent
- seen to be equitable
- recognizes individuals and teams
- has buy-in from recipients
- recognizes specialist skills
- keeps abreast of the market
- rewards essential behaviours
- rewards improvement as well as achievement
- simple to communicate and understand
- flexible enough to generate local relevance.

SETTING BASIC PAY
We have seen that basic pay sets the job in a value matrix, therefore in setting basic pay we must be sure that:
- it is at least equal to the current market value for that work
- it is in the correct relative position to other jobs
- it is accepted as a fair valuation by the job holder.

Time rates

Basic pay is often expressed in terms of hourly rates, weekly pay or annual salaries. At its crudest this means that employees clock in and out and are paid for the time shown on their clock card. This method is rapidly falling into disrepute because it emphasizes that pay is for attending rather than for what is done and it makes a negative differentiation between the on-the-clock employees and those members of staff who are not. It creates a master–servant relationship and encourages people to do as little as possible for their time pay.

In most modern TQ-thinking companies this clock technique has been abandoned. People in employment sell their skills, energies and enthusiasms, not their time. Attendance recording is for safety, security and administrative reasons only and applies universally to all employees, lowest to highest.

Job evaluation

Basic pay is traditionally linked to the job rather than the person. Although it is to be hoped that there will be a movement away from this approach, while basic pay recognizes the relative value of the type of work done in a job it means that a job must be evaluated to set it in the correct position on a value scale. In order to satisfy the requirement of obvious fairness, job evaluation has developed into a very formal structured procedure.

Typically a panel of disinterested but experienced and respected managers and trade union officials (if appropriate) will examine a job according to strict guidelines to identify and score characteristics of the job under headings such as responsibility, resources controlled, skills and knowledge, complexity and conditions. For example:
- Responsibility
    - accountability
    - decision times
    - impact of decisions

- access to guidance
- innovation and creativity
- impact of output.
- Resources controlled
  - number of staff
  - annual budget
  - value of assets
  - production volume
  - turnover.
- Skills and knowledge
  - education and training
  - specialist skills
  - job knowledge
  - analytical
  - judgement
  - people skills
  - technical
  - coaching and facilitation
  - team building and leading
  - communication
  - management.
- Complexity
  - number of units controlled
  - variety of functions and disciplines involved
  - complexity and number of tasks
  - contact with other departments
  - contact with external customers/suppliers
  - contact with community.
- Conditions
  - physical requirements
  - abnormal working (heights, temperature, hazardous materials)
  - extended or abnormal hours of work.

The total score against these considerations will indicate at which point in the pay scale that the job in question is positioned. There are several other named methods of evaluation – for instance, the Urwick–Orr profile method in which the use of knowledge, aptitude and skills is set against a job profile; or the Paterson decision band method in which there are six basic bands from top management, through middle management, skilled to unskilled, with jobs graded by the character of the decisions made within it. For a more comprehensive treatment of these and other methods the reader should refer to a more specialized text (Walker Morris, 1973).

Job evaluation depends for its success on accurate job descriptions. This can be quite difficult to articulate because the incumbents and their supervisors have developed an unspoken understanding of what the job is about, which is difficult to specify. Furthermore, once it is specified, any on-going changes will prompt a return to the evaluation panel.

INCOME IMPROVERS

Band progression
The most elegant way of recognizing performance as described by the appraisal is by increasing the slope of the progression line within the band boundaries.

Rather than a job being on a flat basic rate within the pay scales it is common to allocate pay bands to jobs. This offers the prospect of some income improvement in that, without promotion to a higher-paid job, there can be some progress through the band (Fig. 9.1). Criteria for progression can be:

- Service: each year of service will qualify for another step within the band until the maximum is reached.
- Skills/competence: as skills are improved and added to, so they will be rewarded by progress through the band.
- Performance: performance measures are used to determine the rate of progress through the band.
- A combination of some or all of the above.

A good performance (A) will bring the employee to the top of the scale in

● APPLICATION OF REWARD IN PRACTICE

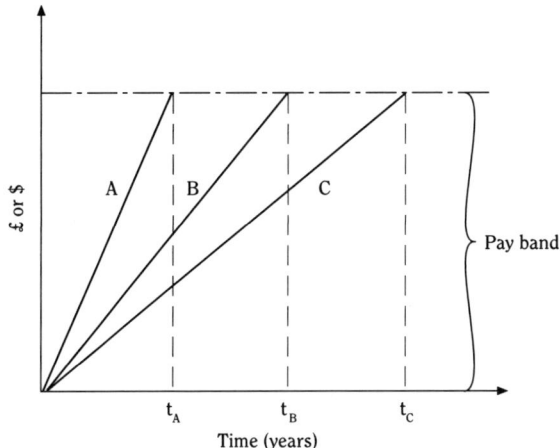

FIGURE 9.1 Pay bands and progress by performance

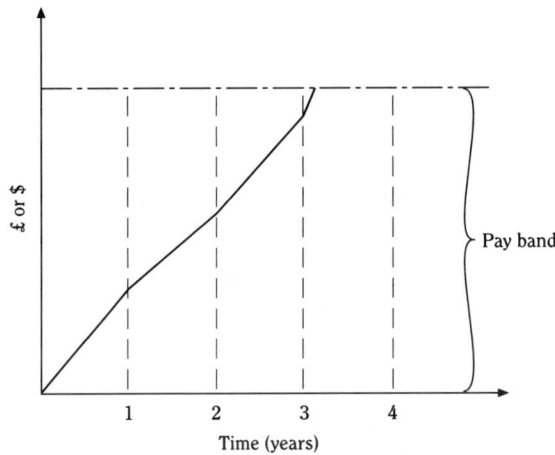

FIGURE 9.2 Pay band – typical progress

the shortest time while less good performances (B, C) will take longer. In reality performance is unlikely to improve constantly with time and a more typical progression would be stepped as in Fig 9.2. The effect of cost of

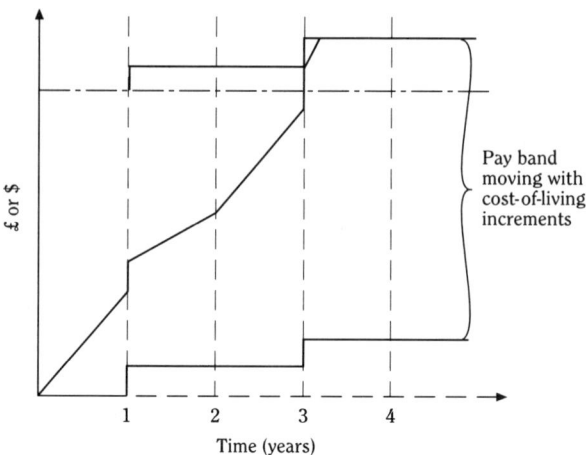

FIGURE 9.3 Pay band – effect of cost-of-living increments

living increases (if given) or employment market forces are coped with by changing the position of the scale, in which case there will be a step change in each pay rate to return to the same relative position on the scale (Fig. 9.3).

There are several important features of these scale systems:

- Unless progress is to be on service alone, they require a form of appraisal of progress. This has been anathema to British trade unions for many years and so the unionized personnel have been excluded from progression by performance.
- All systems involving scales and bands share the common dilemma of, what happens when you reach the top of the band? In some companies, Nissan Motor Manufacturing (UK) Ltd being an example, there is no debate: when you reach the top of the band you reach a plateau and cannot progress further. There is a certain logic in this approach, because if people are paid to do a job then the best that they can expect, however good they are at it, is the maximum rate for that job. There are some cultural difficulties with this argument because the value of the job takes precedence over the value of the person and no further income

improvement is possible without promotion. Thus there is a danger of accumulating groups of the most experienced and skilled employees who are on a plateau and frustrated. There is also a danger that those progressing towards the maximum will feel that the incentive to improve is diminished. These phenomena have prompted the appearance of several modifications to the rigid band structure to minimize these effects.

- Additional service awards: a service bonus usually paid every other year of presence at the scale maximum. These bonuses are one-off and are non-pensionable.
- Special performance increments: above-average and high performers are given a pensionable salary increment, usually less than that given within the band, with which they can continue to make progress within a personal attainment zone.
- Performance bonuses: one-off non-pensionable awards for performance worthy of some recognition.
- Promotion: speed of acquisition of the band maximum is itself a measure of sustained performance and will be a factor influencing the choice of promotion candidates. It is one definition of a high flyer.

Skill-based payments

There are two ways of incorporating skill payments into these systems:

1 Recognized as part of overall performance: the acquisition of a skill will be seen as part of the expected activities of the job and measured against performance accordingly.
2 Recognized as moving the job into a higher pay band.

Either or both can be used, but the former is culturally more elegant, and can look at the application of the acquired skill for producing actual performance.

Teams

Basic pay as a valuation of individuals and their jobs will take into account the value of those jobs within a team or teams. The performance of the individual within the team will influence the judgements about progression through the pay bands. Teams will include members from several different pay bands.

APPRAISAL

The very term reward suggests that it is provided in return for some service, activity or achievement and therefore some form of assessment is implied. As I am advocating that reward should be given not only to the completion of a task but also to the achievement of goals and objectives, the manner in which they are achieved and to the improvement in performance, then clearly it is necessary to review all of this. Indeed annual appraisals are often known as performance reviews.

Appraisal is the window through which individuals can see their performance, it is not an exercise to calculate pay; but it is legitimate for them to see that image reflected in their income. A detailed view of the appropriate appraisal methods is given in Chapter 10.

RESULTS-BASED INCREMENTS

Bonuses

Proponents of bonuses criticize PRP via band progression because the percentage impact on total income is comparatively small (1–5 per cent), hence any motivational effect is diffuse. Bonuses, however, can be sized to have recognizable impact.

The two types of bonus, annual and by-the-event, can be used most effectively if the allocation is delegated to the lowest possible level. That means that line managers, team leaders and supervisors should decide who the recipients are and how much they get.

Funding

Resources are not infinite and there are differences in funding:
- Annual bonuses are commonly provided from a fund approved at the

director level of an organization and allocated to divisions, departments, sites and teams. The fund can be allocated on a per capita basis or by contribution or by achievement. I am an advocate of empowering each level of allocation to choose their own method, but where appropriate I would always incline to performance-related methods. The most securely bound teams may feel able to discuss the allocation openly and publicly.
- By-the-event bonuses have to come out of a department's or team's fixed cost budget and it is important that budget provision is made annually. Delegation of decision is equally valid here as for annual bonuses.

These methods do raise concerns about consistency and the dangers of divisiveness, but I would say that the risks come with the territory of empowerment. They are minimized by the setting of sensible boundaries and by adequate coaching of managers, supervisors and leaders.

At-risk elements

A significant proportion of available income (5 per cent or more) is made conditional on the achievement of pre-agreed targets. This is either a win/no-win arrangement or in some versions percentage achievement can bring proportional reward. The advantages of such schemes are that:

- motivation is strong
- rewards are committed, i.e. if the goals are attained the bonus will be paid
- non-achievement brings a powerful message.

The disadvantages, however, are legion:

- Because it is only those with high basic pay that can afford to put more than 5 per cent of their pay at risk, this method is most often used for senior staff, though there are examples of universal application. This results in large disparities in both performance awards and actual incomes. This in turn leads to secrecy and suspicion.
- Applied to annual targets (and they usually are) these payments promote all the evils of the ends justifying the means and short-termism.
- Because the practice is prevalent among the most senior and influential staff, it can lead to behavioural and hence cultural changes throughout an organization.

- Unless the practice is set up to gauge annual performance only as a contribution to a longer-term (say five-year) goal, it will have a negative effect on TQ cultures.

All in all, unless the strength of the culture is such that it can resist these negative pressures then the method can cause more harm than good.

Gainsharing

This idea has a history rooted in some of the early productivity schemes such as the Scanlon and Rucker plans (see Chapter 7). It links obvious identifiable performance improvement to rewards by sharing the gains created by the improvements. Many of the early successes, especially in the USA were in small and medium-sized operations (up to 1000 employees) and it has been thought that size is a limitation. But the advent of TQ and the perceived need to link reward systems to its culture has prompted some interesting schemes in larger companies as well. We can look at an example from the US operation of BP Chemicals (BPC).

This division measures and compares its performance against three criteria:

1 External competition – the competitive index.
2 Its own performance contracts (target and goals) – division performance.
3 With the rest of BPC – internal ranking.

To calculate the competitive index, operating income is compared to a basket of chemical industry competitors. The percentage change over the year places BPC into a tier within the list of companies. Each tier attracts a competitive index value (Table 9.1).

Similarly for the division performance the comparison is made against targets (financial and non-financial), milestones and objectives (Table 9.2).

Table 9.1 Competitive index

Tier 1	9%
Tier 2	6%
Tier 3	3%
Tier 4	0%

And for the internal ranking, the division's performance is put in a league table with the other BPC divisions (Table 9.3).

TABLE 9.2 Division performance

Above 120% achievement	9%
110–120%	6%
100–110%	3%
Below 100%	0%

TABLE 9.3 Internal ranking

1st	9%
2nd	6%
3rd	3%
4–7th	0%

These three criteria are then weighted (Table 9.4). This effectively makes the point that while actual performance is paramount it must always be put in the context of the competition (internal and external).

TABLE 9.4 Weighted criteria

Competitive index	25%
Division performance	50%
Internal ranking	25%

The final calculation is completed as in Table 9.5. This shows that a gainshare pool worth 6 per cent of the year-end salaries will be established. Fifty per cent of the pool is distributed pro rata to all qualifying employees and the remaining 50 per cent is distributed to function departments and teams based on their own performances. All those employees who have an appraisal rating of E (effective) or above are eligible and the schemes payments are in addition to those paid by the company's PRP system.

TABLE 9.5 Gainshare pool

	RESULT	SCORE	WEIGHTING	AMOUNT
Competitive index	Tier 1	9%	0.25	2.25%
Division performance	115%	6%	0.5	3.0%
Internal ranking	3rd	3%	0.25	0.75%
Total pool				6.0%

Another version of gainsharing has been introduced at BP Exploration's Prudhoe Bay operations in Alaska. There, all employees share in the benefits arising as a result of improvements in production, safety, environmental and cost targets. In this case the measures are very simple and as in the BP Chemicals example there are regular updates of progress through the year. One employee in Alaska wrote that the big win of the scheme was that all employees knew that their performance made a difference; that their performance affected the company's performance.

In France, where such schemes can enjoy tax incentives, there are some interesting examples. There is one called La Participation and another called L'Intéressement, in which a percentage of the benefits of performance improvement are allocated for reward and are distributed 50 per cent to individuals and 50 per cent to teams.

The disadvantages of such schemes are that:
- they are broad in scope and do not recognize the individual contribution
- they share in the gains but not in the losses
- there are some administrative costs.

These are greatly outweighed by the advantages which are that they:
- promote performance improvement
- enhance participation and ownership
- give rewards to individuals and teams
- identify with the performance culture
- encourage communication
- encourage measurement
- create a sense of realism.

They require an open participative culture that extends to all parts of the organization including any unionized parts. There has to be good upward feedback and established active listening. For all of these reasons gainsharing schemes closely align with TQ culture and merit serious consideration.

Profit sharing

In principle, all profit-sharing schemes are similar. Assuming a company is in profit a proportion of the profit is distributed to employees, usually all employees. Most schemes have a condition that requires the profit to reach a declared minimum before sharing can take place. The amount to be distributed is sometimes prescribed in the details of the scheme and sometimes left to the discretion of the directors. Typically the proportion of profits shared out are between 2 and 10 per cent with the majority being in the region 5 to 6 per cent. The amount should be credible without becoming such a significant part of income that it becomes expected and relied upon.

There are two ways of distributing the share, either as cash bonuses, annually or semi-annually, or as stock. ICI was a prominent company to use the stock method. Stock can be issued directly as shares or via an 'approved deferred share trust', by which the profit to be distributed is put in a trust fund which is then used to buy shares in the company on behalf of the employees.

Allocation can be as a percentage of basic pay or of annual earnings. In so far that the latter recognizes all additions and improvements to pay such as skills payments, service payments, overtime and PRP, it is slightly preferable in terms of a fit with the TQ culture.

The disadvantages of profit sharing are that:
- it is the form of performance-related award that is most remote from the influence of the recipient and hence lacks impact
- it is uncommitted, in that high performance may not generate profit
- it is indiscriminate in its application to all employees
- profits can vary significantly and therefore it provides an unreliable source of income.

The benefits of profit sharing are that:

- it recognizes the important contribution of all employees to corporate success
- it relates performance to success
- it creates an awareness of the financial realities of business.

Share schemes

These are devised to encourage share ownership by the workforce and in terms of motivation work in the same way as profit sharing. They offer an incentive to own and retain shares in the employing company. There follows an example that is typical of several schemes.

Eligible employees (that means virtually all employees in the best schemes) are invited to buy shares in the company and lodge them with trustees who retain them for one year. In return the company will issue additional shares to the employees in proportion to their own investment (in many cases this is one share for one share). These additional shares are held by the trustees for a longer period, say five years. During the holding period the shares may not be traded but dividends accrue to the shareholder in the normal way and the value of the retained shares varies with the market. At the end of the holding period unfettered ownership of the shares is transferred to the shareholder.

Such a scheme has no direct link to performance except that the directors will take the overall performance of the company into account when deciding what provision to make and when to make it to fund additional shares.

The disadvantages of this type of scheme are that:
- they are optional and may not involve all employees
- there is no direct link to performance
- they promote the interests of shareholders above other stakeholders
- they are indiscriminate in terms of individual contributions
- they require a financial contribution up-front from the employee
- they are not committed in that frequency and amount of funding are at the discretion of the directors.

The benefits of such schemes are that:
- they apply to all employees

- they encourage a feeling of ownership
- they create awareness of the financial performance of the company
- they encourage loyalty
- there are significant financial benefits to individuals linked to the company's success.

Share options

These are a form of reward involving company shares that is normally limited to the most senior executives and, in some companies, only to directors. The options are decided by the board shortly after the declaration of the half-year and annual results. The option price will be the price at the date of the grant of the option. There will be a limit on the size of the option, both in terms of the aggregated option holding of an individual (say four times salary) and in terms of the total options outstanding relative to the total equity of the company (say not more than five per cent). Options may be exercised after three years from the date of grant but not after ten years.

Here is an example of a share option scheme that is offered to all employees in addition to and in parallel with share ownership schemes. It recognizes that all employees may not have funds available to buy out their options at an optimum time and therefore it is a savings-related share option. The employees enter into a save-as-you-earn contract with nominated savings organizations and are offered the option to take the proceeds of the contract on maturity (five or seven years) in shares at the option price determined by the share value at the time of opening the contract. If the fortunes of the company have prospered during the period of the contract then there will be a financial advantage; this can be multiplied by investing the resultant shares in the participating share scheme.

The disadvantages of option schemes are related to their availability to senior personnel only:
- they are divisive
- they distort differentials
- they conflict with the desired culture

- they can encourage short-term actions to boost share performance
- they promote the interests of shareholders above other stakeholders.

The benefits of option schemes are that:
- they encourage long-term loyalty
- they promote a long-term view of performance
- they relate personal financial advantage to the success of the company
- they motivate to achieve.

THE OVERALL REWARD PACKAGE

In practice a realistic reward package will contain a mix of several, if not most, of the available options. In choosing the constituents one should be guided by what is desirable and necessary to achieve the vital cultural alignment that is required. Alignment is the key if reward is going to contribute to culture change rather than inhibit it.

The key constituents of a reward package are as follows:
- Basic pay bands have to be felt fair with respect to both the internal and external environments.
- Mechanisms to improve pay other than market forces have to be present.
- Pay improvement must be linked to
  - performance
  - skills development and deployment
  - behavioural development
  - service.
- Improvements in pay must be based on formal mechanisms of appraisal.
- Performance-related pay must be committed, not dependent on external factors.
- They must include a way of recognizing special contributions.
- A team's achievements and the work of individuals within teams must be part of the assessment of performance.
- They must promote
  - ownership, participation and involvement
  - awareness of the company and its success
  - long-term goals via milestones rather than short-term targets

● APPLICATION OF REWARD IN PRACTICE

  – loyalty.
- They must be simply understood and clearly and openly communicated
  – sustain reasonable differentials rather than expand them
  – promote cohesion rather than division
  – be universal, i.e. apply to all levels of employees.

A good overall reward scheme may comprise these elements (Fig 9.4):
- Basic pay organized in bands set by evaluation and subject to market adjustment.
- Compensation elements, shift pay, disturbance allowances, overtime pay if appropriate, call-out pay, etc.
- Income improvement through the band dependent on performance (as an individual and within a team), skill development and deployment, behaviour and service.
- Personal attainment provisions for above-average performers at the top of the band.
- Improvement judged on the basis of formal appraisal.
- Performance bonuses (teams and individuals).
- Share scheme with parallel universal share option scheme.
- Performance gainsharing (teams and individuals).
- Promotion recognizing cultural role models.
- Life-sustaining benefits, pension scheme, health insurance, child-care provision, social and sporting facilities and subsidized meals at work.

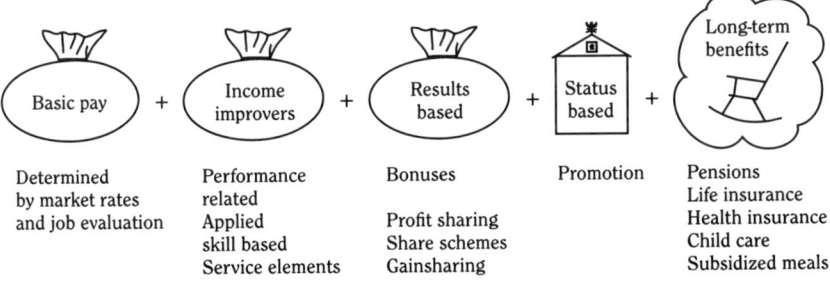

FIGURE 9.4 Elements of a good reward system

Summary
Characteristics of working reward schemes aligned to TQ are:
1 Basic pay
   - time rates
   - job evaluation to establish scales.
2 Income improvers
   - bands within the scales
   - progress through the bands by performance, skills development and deployment, behaviour and service
   - provision for those on the top of the band
   - skill payments
   - teams.
3 Appraisal
   - review of performance for individuals
   - linking of PRP to performance improvement.
4 Results-based increments
   - the allocation and funding of annual and by-the-event bonuses
   - the negative effects of at-risk pay
   - the practical advantages and disadvantages of profit sharing and share schemes (participating and share options)
   - the beneficial practice and cultural advantage of gainsharing.
5 The overall package
   - key constituents
   - the make-up of a good package.

Measures of performance

If we do not measure what we do, how do we know that we are improving? Measurement is close to the heart of any TQ process and phrases like 'What gets measured, gets done', and 'No action without measurement', roll off the tongue.

There are forms of measurement that are based on the rate of working, how much in how long; for example:
- measured day work
- time and motion study
- piece work
- yield bonuses.

Most of them include a standard and are based on the application of prescribed methods with no provision for innovation or improvement, and it is not my intention to discuss them here. Rather I want to concentrate on measures of performance and especially performance improvement within a TQ culture. These measures will include the apparently hard and quantitative such as production, productivity and financial results, and the soft and subjective like customer satisfaction, job satisfaction and behaviour. Measurements are sometimes based on variable data (e.g. temperature, volume, cash flow, etc.) or attributes (correct vs not correct, faults per batch, overweight or underweight) and they will include measures of outputs and inputs, and sometimes combinations to assess the

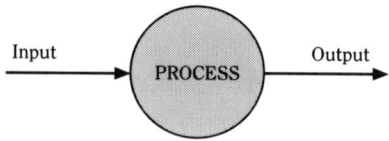

FIGURE 10.1 The process model

performance of the overall process (Fig. 10.1). Measurements will be for companies, businesses, sites, offices, teams and individuals.

PROGRESS OF THE TQ PROCESS

If measurement is at the centre of TQ, it follows that the TQ process itself should be measured. Philip Crosby (1979) had an easy solution on the face of it, in his *Cost of Quality* and more particularly in his *Price of Nonconformance* (PONC), however, some have found that these measures can be over-simplistic in concept, bureaucratic in practice and even misleading. Yet some form of measurement is essential.

Assessment

The most effective answer is some form of assessment format that can not only measure the outputs of the process (e.g. PONC) but the inputs as well, in other words it gives an overall view. The other essential is that the assessment can be repeated at intervals in a consistent, comparable way. To satisfy this requirement it is necessary to use some form of model. The most commonly used models are those based on the criteria for the Baldrige or EQA (EFQM, 1994b) awards (see Chapter 5). The EFQM model is shown in Fig. 10.2. The advantage of such models is that profiles can be developed to indicate strengths, weaknesses and progress against the various categories. The scores can also be used to make and learn from comparisons, both internal and external, in fact to benchmark (see below) the TQ process.

Each of the categories can be examined by means of a questionnaire that will produce a category score; an example is given in Fig. 10.3.

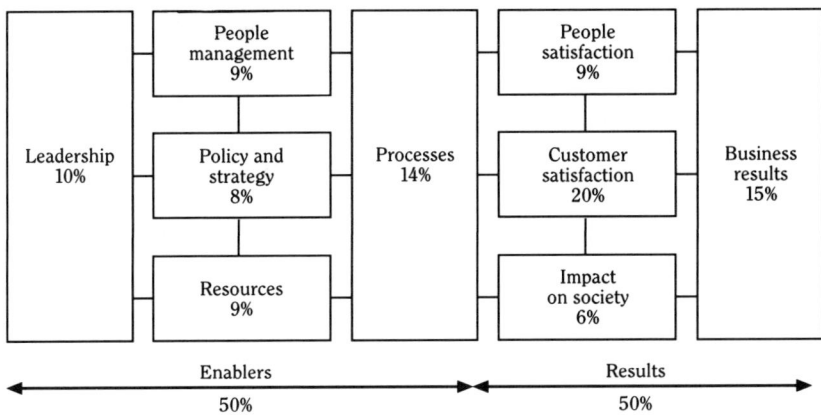

FIGURE 10.2   EFQM model
Source: EFQM

There are other assessment models that can be used effectively, but they should be checked for alignment against one or other of these that are now assuming the status of standards.

Self-assessment

There are many consultants who will be happy to offer their services to assess your process in this way. Even if a consultant is used to introduce and establish the technique, for reasons of economy, involvement and ownership of the results the ultimate aim should be self-assessment. Not surprisingly, it is possible to purchase customized software if electronic methods seem appropriate.

OUTPUTS

The pure Deming approach to quality management (Deming, 1982) would suggest that we should not put too much emphasis on measuring outputs because, provided we measure what is going on in the process, the outputs will look after themselves. I would not be so categorical and, as we have seen, the EQA criteria for assessing excellence in quality management sets

MOTIVATING YOUR ORGANIZATION

The management of the organization's employees and how it releases their full potential to improve its business continuously.

1. The skills and capabilities of employees are preserved and developed through recruitment, training and career progression by:
   - defining and comparing people skills with the organizations requirements
   - planning recruitment and advancement
   - establishing training plans, implementing and monitoring effectiveness
   - developing employees following initial induction training

2. Employees are involved in the establishment of agreed personal and departmental targets and that performance relative to these is continuously monitored and reviewed through an appraisal system.

3. The involvement of every employee in continuous improvement teams is encouraged and promoted and employees are empowered to implement improvement actions e.g. promotion can be via in-house conferences and meetings.

4. There are specific methods of promoting employee improvement contributions such as an effective suggestion scheme.

5. Employees are rewarded for innovation.

6. Effective top-down and bottom-up communication is achieved via regular two-way briefings.

7. The organization's human resources strategy plan supports the policy and strategy of the business.

8. Surveys of the organization's employee perceptions are used to assess continuous improvement on people management.

Total

FIGURE 10.3   People management, nine per cent weighting

50 per cent of the score against results. In the USA, The Malcolm Baldrige award allocates 18 per cent of its score.

In looking at output measures it is important to choose them in the context of the receiver of the output. The quality awards mentioned above refer to companies. The EFQM suggests that there are four receivers of

● MEASURES OF PERFORMANCE

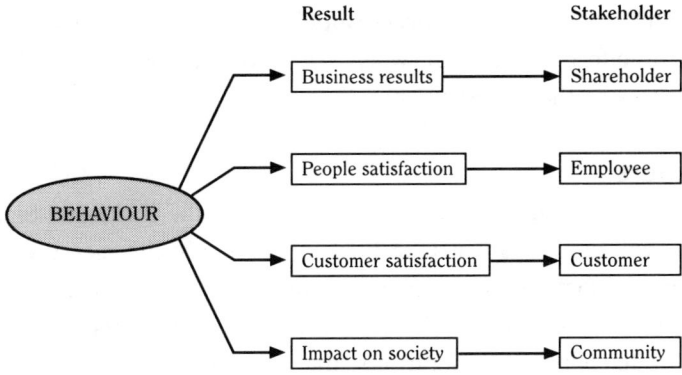

FIGURE 10.4 Indicators of TQ performance

output from a company – I prefer the term stakeholders – and each of them will be interested in a different set of measures, a different set of results (see Fig. 10.4).

Shareholders

Shareholders are interested in financial results:

1 *Return on capital employed* gives a measure of the efficiency of use of the financial resources available.
2 *Internal rate of return* is the application of financial efficiency measures to the internal operations of the company, excluding external financial effects.
3 *Cash flow* or funds flow (includes capital investment) is the pattern of movement of cash in and out of a business, indicating the peak borrowing needs.
4 *Profit* is simply the difference between receipts and outgoings for a specified time period; it is sales revenue less all costs.
5 *Sales per employee* is an example of an index that can be tracked over time and compared department to department and business to business. Although it can be used to measure the effectiveness of a sales

department when the employees would be those in the department, it is also an effective indicator when used company-wide with the total employees as the denominator.

Customers

Customers are those who receive the products of the processes. Since the quality revolution began to take hold in the 1980s the measurement of customer satisfaction has become a growth industry. More and more companies are researching into the views of their customers using either written or telephone questionnaires, the most assiduous contacting each customer for feedback after the completion of every order. It is almost impossible to stay in a hotel without being asked to fill in a customer survey form. It is also important to survey potential customers and former customers to ascertain why they are going elsewhere.

As well as surveys, there are other measures:

1 *Customer complaints* are an indication but are never enough alone.
2 *On time in full* (OTIF) deliveries is a fundamental measure of conformance to customer requirements. Some companies that have measured this for the first time have had a very severe shock – some even recording zero per cent.
3 *Customer retention* is in many ways the most significant measure. If a customer comes back for repeat orders he or she must be satisfied. It also costs many times the cost of servicing an existing customer to win a new one.
4 *Order processing time*. How long does it take from receipt of order to be in a position to deliver? How does that compare with the competition? How can it be improved?
5 *Performance of the sales office* from the customer's perception may be an important feature of the relationship. Do they respond courteously and effectively? Are they knowledgeable about the products, prices and deliveries? Are they aware of the customer's special needs? All of this is measured by asking the customers to comment and score it, say 0 to 10.
6 *Invoice processing time and accuracy* is important to customers too. The supplier's invoice has to fit into the customer's accounting system; if

they appear erratically or have errors it will cost the customer more to deal with it.

As regards the customers, they are interested in value and *performance of the product or service.*

Value = Price + cost of doing business

It is the *cost of doing business* term that plays a large part in the satisfaction of a customer. It is sometimes called the hassle factor but when the order to delivery process goes wrong, it costs the customer something as well as the supplier. All of these measures have to be presented in a form in which improvement can be monitored (see key performance indicators, page 127). At car rental specialists Avis, bonuses of up to 20 per cent can be paid, 50 per cent of which is based on customer survey results and the remainder on financial performance, while at Xerox in the UK 20 per cent of the senior management bonus relates to customer satisfaction.

Employees

The satisfaction of the employees is often overlooked as a measure of the performance of an organization, but the best and most consistent performers in terms of shareholders and customers will also score highly in this category. Therefore, as with customers, we must ask the employees questions about their work and their relationship with, and opinions of, the company. Properly constructed employee surveys can be extremely informative and often provide management with an entirely new perspective on their company.

The survey questions should test:
- awareness of the company's mission, strategy, goals and milestones
- effectiveness of communication, up and down
- understanding of the improvement ethic and culture (e.g. TQM)
- opportunities for improvement
- customer focus
- understanding of specific policies (e.g. employment, environment)
- relationships with line management

- the variation of opinion and satisfaction at different levels in the company
- satisfaction with:
  - the reward system and package
  - the appraisal system
  - training
  - career development
  - job content
  - teamworking
  - welfare issues.

These surveys can be carried out in different ways, for instance:

- Through the internal mail they may be distributed to all employees, who are invited to complete and return them at their leisure. This system will produce an incomplete response, typically between 50 and 70 per cent, and the response may be distorted in different levels of the organization.
- Formal facilitated sessions may be held in which a work group, team or department will sit together for an hour to fill in the questionnaire. The purpose and design of the questionnaire can be explained and ambiguities about specific questions can be dealt with. The benefit of this approach is that it gives a consistent high response (90 per cent) and there are fewer doubts about the interpretation of questions.

Whichever system is employed there are certain essential points:

- the purpose of the survey must be thoroughly communicated
- the survey should be universal with all employees asked the same questions
- the results should be professionally and independently analysed
- the results should be openly communicated to all with full explanations of the significance of the findings with particular reference to the rate of improvement that they represent
- feedback on the results should be sought
- a resultant action plan should be drawn up.

There are other indicators of employee satisfaction that can be used on shorter time scales than surveys, such as turnover, absenteeism, sickness rates, safety statistics, and ease of recruitment.

To track performance improvement in this area an index can be developed including some or all of the features above while the survey repeated, say, every two years can be constructed in such a way that each group of questions can be scored in terms of percentage satisfaction.

In the UK there is a new initiative called 'Investors in People' (see also Chapter 11) which measures an organization's investment in the training and development of its people against a national standard; however there is no direct measurement of employee satisfaction implied.

Community

By community is meant the geographic area in which a business exists: its environment, life and people. The commercial life is as much a part of the community as the social interaction of its people. Of course, industry and commerce have a direct impact with noise, pollution and traffic as well as the wealth that is created. In a way the community is the receiver of these outputs and it can be treated as the customer, with the full weight of the quality process being brought to bear to improve its satisfaction.

Noise, pollution and traffic are all variables that can be measured quantitatively, but it is the perception of the community (customer satisfaction) that matters. With these issues, this perception is often created at the emotional level rather than from factual data. To change this it is necessary to create relationships of trust by openly sharing with the community the policy objectives, targets, milestones and actual current performance in this area – the unvarnished, undiluted truth! For example, in BP Chemicals a policy of public disclosure was adopted in 1992, with the actual tonnage of effluents and emissions being disclosed openly to communities and the media. The proposed targets for improvement were also revealed with an undertaking to report progress openly and regularly in the future.

There are some further attribute measures of impact on the community that are of value – for instance, reportable incidents (operational safety), educational links, positive press comment, etc.

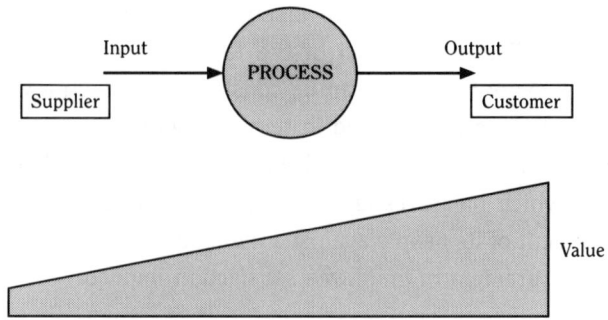

FIGURE 10.5 The process model and value improvement

INPUTS

In order to measure the contribution of performance to all those activities that create an output we must first understand their interrelationships; in fact we need to understand the nature of a process with value being added between input and output (Fig 10.5).

Processes

To carry out processes, employees or teams will need job knowledge and skills, they will have to work to a design, procedure or specification, they will have to have training and to behave in ways that are consistent with the improvement culture and in particular with a drive to improve the process. Each of these aspects can themselves be improved and the improvement can be measured.

Key business processes

Individual processes join together to become a process chain, the output of one supplying the input of another and so on, with value being added across the chain (Fig. 10.6). In fact the processes can be complex with many decision nodes, alternative paths and recycles, and analysis of them can form the basis for significant improvement. A very simple example is shown

● MEASURES OF PERFORMANCE

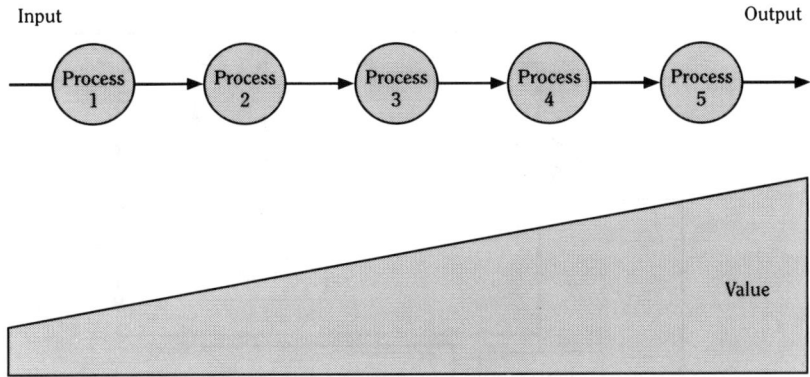

FIGURE 10.6 The process chain and value improvement

in Fig. 10.7; in practice these process charts are extremely complex and can often cover a whole wall!

Any business will have numerous chains but for performance measurement to be linked to the strategic focus of a company then those processes that are key to delivering that strategy must be identified. Most businesses will identify between four and ten such key processes, for example:

- The supply chain or customer order process, from receipt of order through materials supply, production, distribution, delivery, invoicing to receipt of payment.
- Innovation, from market research through technical research, development, to launch and commercialization of a new product.
- Customer management, from initial contact through capture, retention, relationship building, involvement, feedback and resultant action, to anticipating new product needs.
- People management, from recruitment through training, development, team building, core competences, reward and recognition, coaching and facilitated learning to continuously improving contribution.
- Capital management, from the identified investment opportunity through project review, outline design, costing, value engineering, proposal,

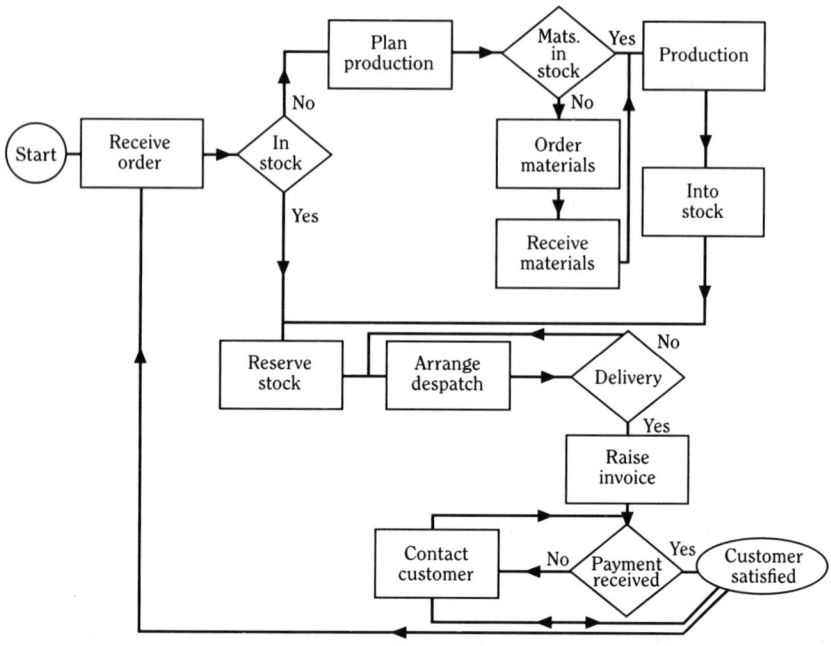

FIGURE 10.7　A process map

approval, allocation of funds, project implementation, construction, commissioning to financial review and feedback.

The performance of those operating these processes can be related, of course, to customer satisfaction but also to the maximum satisfaction of the other stakeholders. Improvements can be measured in factors such as lead times, cycle times, added value, costs and reduction of environmental impact.

Recognition of performance in the delivery and support of these key processes gives powerful endorsement to the strategic and cultural direction of a company.

Process capability

Is it possible for the process that has been constructed to deliver what is required? The reader with an aversion to statistical techniques should be reassured at this point that I shall leave the mathematical explanations to more specialized texts (see Oakland and Followell, 1990). But everyone needs to understand at least one of the terms.

The *Process Capability Index* (Cp) is a measure of how much of the product of a process is likely to be produced within the specification limits:
- Cp = 1 means that 99.7% of the output will conform
- Cp < 1 means that significant non-conforming product will arise from the process
- CP > 1 means that all product will conform and that there is some room for variation of process conditions.

The Gaussian distribution curve (Fig. 10.8) describes the occurrence of product around the mean desired value; at Cp = 1, 99.7 per cent of its width is 6σ (where σ, sigma, is the statistical standard deviation). This gives rise to the term 'Six Sigma Quality' used to good effect by some companies as a rallying slogan for their TQ process. Motorola, for example, have used it widely to set strategic targets.

Measurement of performance against capability targets is a direct measure of improvement and potential improvement.

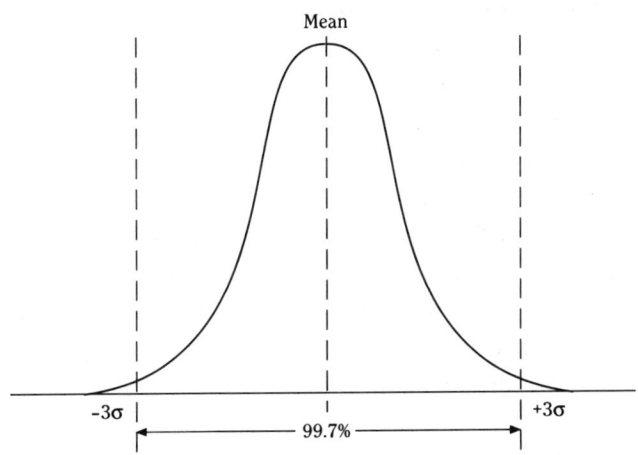

FIGURE 10.8 Process capability-distribution curve

Process control

The day-to-day monitoring of processes can be used to measure improvement by using attributes such as the number of excursions outside control limits, or the tightening of control limits as the process comes under improved control.

Quality assurance

Quality assurance (QA) is about conformance to prescribed procedures which, if followed, will produce the desired quality of product. Measurement of adherence to those procedures is by audit, internal and external. There are attributes that can be linked to performance: for example, the number of deficiencies reported, the number of corrective actions identified and the number completed since the last audit.

Benchmarking

Benchmarking relies on measurement. It is a measured comparison with others carrying out similar processes. It can be grouped into three types:

1 *Internal.* Many organizations have more than one department or group or team doing the same or similar operations. Benchmarking between them provides opportunities for open and honest learning and a framework for performance rewards.
2 *Competitive.* The specific comparison of key business processes with competitors. Both parties in the exercise must recognize that there is potential for beneficial learning from each other. Care must be exercised to conduct the comparison in such a way as not to breach any anti-trust or unfair trading legislation.
3 *Functional.* Particular functions in an organization are compared to similar functions in another company. The selection of the benchmarking partner should be on the basis of the 'best in class' operator in the function of interest.

   For instance, the function may be distribution, in which case one would try to partner with a recognized 'best in class' distribution company; or it may be invoice processing in which case one would select a partner for whom that was a key process.

As well as benchmarking the key processes it is possible to compare outputs, competences, customer satisfaction, strategies and even reward and recognition.

Effective benchmarking identifies the 'best in class' and hence the gap between their performance and your own. Improvement performance can be measured by the amount of closure of that gap. It is unlikely that the gap will be the same across all activities in the process chain. It is also true that the 'best in class' title may not attach to the same company for each activity. Hence it is helpful to draw up a profile (Fig 10.9).

The 'activities' are actually the inputs that generate the overall outputs (results) of the complex process of the business. Hence in TQ terms this technique is very healthy in that it concentrates on potential improvements in the way that things are accomplished rather than what is accomplished.

A recent study of supply chain management by a group of over 20 leading manufacturing companies in the UK (Inter Company Productivity Group, 1993) used this profiling technique in a mutual benchmarking exercise and profiled themselves on a scale of A to E (with A representing poor and E, excellent). Each of these scale ratings can be characterized by a description of activities typical for that status. Each participating company was able to draw its own profile and compare it with the group profile, and thus identify those areas to which to apply resources to achieve maximum gap closure with 'best in class'. The technique was used to profile the relative performance of the constituent processes in the supply chain and their support processes including performance measurement and reward and recognition (see. Fig. 10.9).

Benchmarking, gap management and this profiling technique depend on the exercise being repeated at intervals to achieve a measure of improvement performance.

Support activities

Key business processes require to be supported by other processes and systems such as training, information technology, communication and corrective action and there will be appropriate measures in all of these areas.

MOTIVATING YOUR ORGANIZATION

		A	B	C	D	E
Organization	1 Accountability for supply chain			●		
	2 Clarity of structure				●	
	3 Horizontal integration				●	
	4 Ownership and commitment			●		
Resource management	1 Business planning			●		
	2 Optimizing the supply chain				●	
	3 Cost management			●		
	4 Outsourcing				●	
Inventory management	1 Accuracy of inventory		●			
	2 Control of inventory		●			
	3 Inventory losses			●		
Information technology and systems	1 Degree of integration			●		
	2 Development of systems		●			
	3 Electronic data interchange				●	
	4 Systems introduction			●		
Continuous improvement	1 Improvement strategy			●		
	2 Improvement objectives		●			
	3 Improvement teams			●		
	4 Learning processes				●	
	5 Training			●		
	6 Recognition and reward			●		
Performance measurement			●			

FIGURE 10.9 Benchmarking profile
Source: Inter Company Productivity Group – John Russell Associates

Metrics

Systems of measurement have to be devised that have these characteristics:
- understood by all
- readily comparable across teams, functions, businesses and companies
- will add value to crude data
- will relate to the strategic direction of the company
- well accepted with good ownership
- free from corruption by external factors.

Key performance indicators

In looking at the performance of the key business processes, indicators of the performance of the process must be defined. Camp (1989) emphasizes that the success of benchmarking is dependent on selecting the correct performance indicators; for example, in the supply chain process there will be indicators of:

- output ... te/day
- productivity ... te/man
- equipment reliability ... %, defined as
$$\frac{\text{hours in productive operation} \times 100}{\text{available hours} - \text{hours lost for market reasons}}$$
- Conversion costs ... £/te, defined as variable costs less raw materials costs
- stores ... £s of inventory value
- distribution ... % on time in full deliveries
- transport ... £/te mile.

For customer satisfaction there will be an index which will include these factors:
- customer complaints
- sales office performance
- on time in full deliveries
- order processing time
- invoice processing
- repeat orders.

Experience curves

The key performance indices can be plotted over time, often over a period of years, to show the impact of initiatives and to learn the lessons. In looking back over the 1980s one company plotted these indices and saw that in response to the recession of 1980–82 it had cut costs vigorously, not only people costs but operating costs such as maintenance. When in 1986 the economic upturn was in full cry, production fell short of demand because of poor reliability, and people costs escalated, apparently uncontrolled. These lessons helped shape the approach to the recession of the early 1990s.

If possible it is revealing to plot your curves against those for the 'best in class' because they will indicate the kind of improvement effort required to achieve 'best in class' status yourself. If there is a significant gap to close, continuous improvement of the *kaizen* kind alone will not be enough: some step changes will be needed as well (Fig. 10.10).

Paul O'Neill, Chairman of ALCOA, has said, 'Continuous improvement is exactly the right idea if you are a world leader ... it is probably a disastrous idea if you are far behind in the world standard'. If this is what is required then performance-related reward must reflect that imperative.

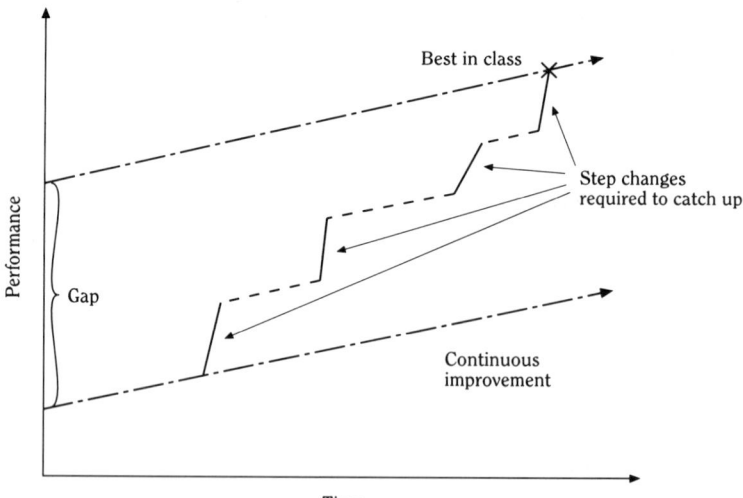

FIGURE 10.10   Progress to 'best-in-class'

Defect measures

These align closely with the 'right first time' philosophy of TQM. They apply particularly to batch and assembly line operations. The number of batches that required no re-work, or the percentage of cars off the line defect-free or once-through are examples of such measures. In the best assembly operations the once-through rate will be over 98 per cent.

These simple measures can have a disproportionate cultural impact. A chemical factory using batch processes had no history of such measurements; when the manager was asked why, he explained that adjusting the 'crude' product by a series of innovative techniques was part of their stock-in-trade. They were developed skills that they were quite proud of – they had become part of the culture and had never been costed. The introduction of this simple metric with a chart on the wall in each building had a remarkable effect.

Price of non-conformance

Crosby (1979) held that the best measurement of improvement was money and the metric he chose was the Price of Non-conformance. This can be regarded as the destruction of value by getting things wrong. This was a constituent of the Cost of Quality (see Fig. 10.11). The PONC can be calculated by such elements as the works cost of producing scrap product, the people costs in getting things wrong, time costs, loss of sales revenue, consequential losses, etc.

Naturally in the Price of Conformance I would include reward and recognition. The danger of this approach is that it is tempting to construct a set of PONC accounts that are parallel to and incompatible with the regular accounts, which leads to confusion and poor acceptability.

Comparisons

Comparisons can be useful with all of these metrics, not only in a formal benchmarking exercise, but also by open and honest comparison of freely published data within a company. These comparisons can be between the performance of individuals, teams, functions or businesses, and if they are

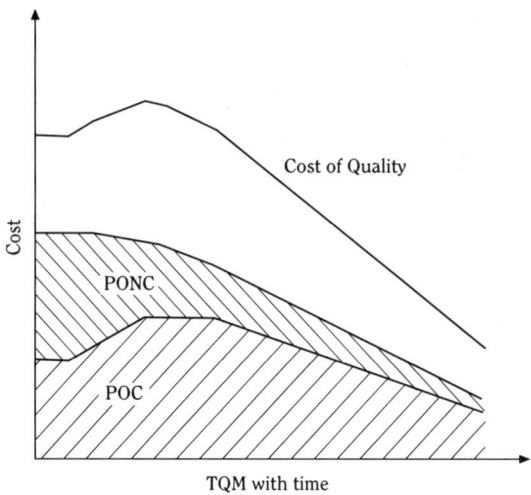

FIGURE 10.11   Cost of quality

not to be divisive they must be made in a culture of mutual learning rather than one of competition. The use of the competitive spirit as a motivator is difficult to sustain and is essentially short-term.

GOAL SETTING

The measurement of performance implies that we are looking for improvement or progress towards some goal or objective. Many performance measures relate to achievement set against those goals. Goal setting is an integral and vital part of the performance improvement – measurement – and reward system.

Vicky Wright and Liz Brading, management consultants, writing on performance-related pay, suggest that one of the features of best practice in this area is that there should be less focus on retrospective performance and more concentration on planning for future improvement (Wright and Brading, 1992). The process of goal setting is the most practical implementation of this assertion.

● MEASURES OF PERFORMANCE

Chapter 1 discussed the place of goals in motivation, and I suggested that there should be clear linkage between an individual's goals and the goals of the company. Similarly, in measuring the progress towards goals, the connection should be made between the measured performance and the performance of the company.

The setting of sensible attainable goals that clearly contribute to the key business processes is an essential step in the reward system. Stretched goals which are, at first sight, unattainable also have their place but are best used to motivate teams, businesses or companies rather than individuals.

Set goals should have these features:
- They should be agreed and not imposed.
- They should be owned and if possible they should be devised by the individual to whom they are to be given.
- They must relate to the team and business goals and to the corporate strategy.
- They must be obviously relevant to the key business processes or their support.
- They must always include targets for improvements as well as absolute targets.
- They must be quantitative and where possible describe what is to be done in measurable terms.
- Where possible they should be time-based, they should refer to frequency, or deadlines, or milestones for longer-term objectives.
- They should be challenging in both content and time while retaining a sense of reality.
- They should develop from success and learn from failure.

Here are a few examples:
- Continue to improve production costs by £x/te by the end of June and by £y/te by the year end.
- Reduce reporting time for monthly accounts from six working days to four by quarter three.
- Complete training in Statistical Process Control by the end of March and develop three applications by the end of September.
- Improve the customer satisfaction index by at least four points in the first half-year.

- Set up regular team meetings, hold at least eight this year with at least one session of upward feedback by the year end.
- During the year reduce cycle time in the customer order process by z per cent.
- To progress its mission to be a world-class supplier in this sector the corporate targets for this year are:
  - To improve profitability by a per cent; return on capital to be at least b per cent with funds flow positive.
  - Customer satisfaction will increase by at least five points, with OTIF (on time in full) being better than 97 per cent.
  - Production reliability will increase to better than 96 per cent and production costs will be reduced by £10/te.
  - The policy to form partnerships with suppliers will continue with the establishing of term contracts with the maintenance contractors.
  - The effluent and emission load will reduce to better than c tes this year. There will be three community liaison meetings and the link activities will be expanded to a further two schools. The policy of open house to the press will be continued.
  - The programme of coaching for team leaders will be extended to the remaining departments.
  - Company-wide communication of the employee survey results will be completed in eight weeks, departments will submit their resulting action plans by the end of April.

Behaviour

This is the great soft issue that apparently presents problems of measurement, but there are techniques that bring a degree of objectivity to otherwise subjective judgements.

Absolute standards

As a general rule rigid standards are not helpful in performance measurements, but in defining its required behaviours, a company will have to set some boundaries of what is acceptable – beyond those

boundaries are no-go areas and so they can be said to be absolute standards. They will refer to such issues as:
- confidentiality
- commercial practices
- acceptance of gifts
- intellectual property
- discrimination
- sexual or racial harassment
- business ethics

in fact, those areas where a breach could seriously damage the reputation and threaten the values of the organization. Within these boundaries the behaviour patterns that affect performance and shape the culture have to be defined and assessed.

Essential behaviours

If the culture is to thrive and performance is to improve, certain behaviours are seen as essential and can be defined. For example, in BP they use the acronym OPEN:
- Open thinking
- Personal impact
- Empowering
- Networking

These can be defined:

O *Open thinking* is the willingness to see others' point of view, to receive new ideas and to challenge traditional thinking. The open thinker will make the right connections and identify key issues.

P *Personal impact* is that behaviour that has a bias for action, is not put off by risk, sees problems as a challenge rather than as a barrier.

E *Empowering* behaviour accepts the responsibility to coach and develop others to fully contribute to team success and gives feedback and support. It understands how to set shared, relevant goals and to implant actions. It can judge when to ask for assistance.

N *Networking* is characterized by an employee who will influence others by expressing positive and negative opinions, who will seek out common interests and communicate frequently to share experience and achievement.

There are many more such definitions, some of which are shown in Fig. 10.12. Many companies will have similar lists and definitions; for example, Nissan Motor Manufacturing (UK) has those shown in Fig. 10.13. For their senior management appraisal they add judgement, decision making, contribution to corporate management and staff development.

To make assessments against all of these definitions, as well as subjective comments, it is possible to locate a relative position of compliance with the definition between strong and weak. Some, as in the Nissan case, provide further description to identify those positions. In fact what is being described by these definitions is a role model for the perfect quality behaviour within those company cultures. We are measuring a profile of the individual's approach to that model.

OTHER SOFT ISSUES

There are other aspects of performance that seem only to be able to be assessed by opinion rather than measurement but in fact in some cases measurements can be devised. For example, British Airways had discerned that an important aspect of customer satisfaction was the cleanliness of the aircraft cabins so they set about measuring the performance of their cleaners. They had to devise a set of metrics, some of which were attributes and some variable measurements. They measured the number of items of foreign bodies discovered on inspection. They developed a white-glove test in which a white-gloved hand was rubbed over surfaces and upholstery to detect contamination and so on.

APPRAISAL PROCEDURE

With all the possible measurement factors given above, there has to be some procedure for bringing them together to assess the overall performance. This is the appraisal procedure (see also Chapter 9). It is

MEASURES OF PERFORMANCE

DEFINITION
Open thinking Radical thinker challenges old ideas and traditional thinking. Can see connections and patterns that others do not. Quickly identifies key issues in complex problems. Open to others' original ideas.
Bias for action Looks to the future, and seeks opportunities and new ideas. Undaunted by risks and difficulty. Anticipates problems and uses many sources in order to clarify and solve them.
Knows what makes others tick Takes time to understand people, gets to know their standpoint, their needs and concerns. Knows how to motivate. Encourages others to talk and express themselves.
Concern for impact Considers impact of action on others, builds respect and trust for actions. Changes behaviour to suit the situation.
Self-confidence Confident of ability, will take on challenge and accept responsibility for success or failure. Willing to evaluate own role and behaviour.
Coaching and developing Accepts responsibility and encourages commitment to developing others. Sets realistic contracts, gives clear feedback, monitors progress, provides support.
Building team success Makes clear contribution to the team. Encourages joint decisions and problem solving. Anticipates and resolves conflict and gives clear roles.
Motivating Uses individual's strengths. Knows what motivates individuals and uses this to get the best out of people. Varies style and mode of encouragement.
Influencing others Unafraid of expressing negative opinions but emphasizes common interests and uses other people where necessary to add further weight.
Reaching others Provides information, makes plans clear. Listens to others and adjusts approach accordingly – ensures understanding. Paints a clear and imaginative picture.
Sharing achievement Communicates frequently and clearly. Clarifies deadlines. Shares vision. Shares success.

FIGURE 10.12 Essential behaviours – definitions
Source: BP Chemicals

2 PERSONAL CHARACTERISTICS

Flexibility

Rigid and inflexible	Not very flexible	Acceptable flexibility	Welcomes new methods and tasks	Constantly seeking to increase personal flexibility
☐	☐	☐	☐	☐

Teamworking

Always seeks to involve others	Works well as a team member	Makes good effort	Dislikes team working	A total loner
☐	☐	☐	☐	☐

Persistence

Positively persists	Fully determined	Can be dissuaded	Rarely persists	Persists to point of awkwardness
☐	☐	☐	☐	☐

Creativity/initiative

Dislikes change	Does not initiate	Welcomes new initiatives	Regularly seeks improvements	Too ready to introduce change
☐	☐	☐	☐	☐

Attendance/timekeeping

100% attendance Never late	Only absent/late when beyond control	Some improvement possible	Has been criticized for attendance/timekeeping	
☐	☐	☐	☐	

Leadership

An outstanding leader	Leads well on most occasions	Does lead at appropriate times	Does not normally lead	Not at all a leader
☐	☐	☐	☐	☐

Persuasiveness

Rarely able to convince others	Achieves a balance	Mostly able to convince others	Always able to convince others	
☐	☐	☐	☐	

Ability to work under pressure

Thrives on pressure	Works well under pressure	Accepts pressure without difficulty	Prefers relaxed atmosphere	Positively dislikes pressure
☐	☐	☐	☐	☐

FIGURE 10.13 Personal characteristics
Source: Nissan Motor Manufacturing (UK)

usually carried out annually and is the link between performance measurement and performance-related reward.

Formality

Of course managers who know their staff should be appraising them all of the time and communicating their thoughts. I recall approaching one of my own appraisal interviews with a formidable boss with some trepidation. I had rehearsed several responses to various imagined incisive comments. When I sat in his office he said, 'What shall we talk about?' I said that I had expected this to be an appraisal interview. 'Yes, but you know my views about you and your work – I would soon tell you if I didn't like anything about the way you went about it.' In fact, I was not at all sure about what he thought about me and my work.

The point is that appraisal must be a matter of systematic review and not based on *ad hoc* impressions. Reward is to be used as an important lever for motivation and therefore it deserves to be based on carefully thought-through formal assessments, with an appropriate allocation of management time.

The formal, systematic approach provides the consistency required of any management system that is going to impact on pay and must be seen to be fair.

Top down

The conventional, well-tried and effective system is for the immediate line manager to make the formal assessment with some checking input from the 'grandparent' manager. The line manager should also seek the views of other managers, particularly those who are 'customers' for the appraisee's work. The interview is carried out by the line manager.

There are some problems that are common to these systems:
- Some managers are not good at it – it is vital that they are coached to a minimum standard before they embark on the exercise.
- There has to be a reasonably interactive relationship between manager and employee – they must be comfortable talking to each other.

- As judgement is involved, it will be subjective. This must be mitigated by including as much quantitative comment as possible to create a reinforcing climate for the subjective judgements.
- 'Big brother' and 'tell' can be characteristics of an appraisal and should be counteracted by introducing as much involvement and participation as possible into the process.
- Some managers are selective with the evidence of the review. They often have their own preconceived mental picture of the individual they are assessing and will seek to reinforce that unbalanced interpretation and wishful thinking.
- The manager may not be technically qualified to judge some of the work, in which case he or she should seek comments from suitably qualified managers.
- The 'grandparent' comments must have credibility based on knowledge of the individual. If they have never met, it is better that comment is avoided as remarks made from apparent ignorance will be resented.

Bottom up

Bottom-up appraisal, sometimes called upward feedback, is much less common but is a feature of open empowered cultures. But it is more than just symbolism, it can be extremely effective. If it is a formal part of the appraisal process it allows constructive criticism of a manager's style, work method, administration and control which is helpful to both parties. And, of course, it forces there to be an interactive conversation. In my experience it is not used as a platform on which to grind axes or vent cynicism; but if it is, there can be no better way to ventilate these negative thoughts and defuse them.

Bottom-up appraisal can take several forms. In one the appraisees are invited to write down their comments about the manager, the comments will be discussed at the appraisal interview and are a matter of record. Another technique is much more public and requires there to be strongly built teams; in this the team meets and the leader invites open comment on his or her performance. This is followed up in later sessions with a review of the improvement of the leader's performance.

An example
Here is an idealized example of an appraisal process based on the BP Chemicals model.

Step 1
Before the beginning of each appraisal period (usually the calendar year) a list of objectives is agreed (see Fig. 10.14). These will include some that are:
- common to most employees and provide a vehicle for guidance in a particular cultural or strategic direction, e.g.:
  - 'Appraise, coach, counsel and develop staff to help them improve performance throughout the year.'
  - 'Contribute to registration to ISO 9000.'
  - 'Improve overall safety performance to achieve a 3 rating on the International Safety Rating System (ISRS) scale.'
- results-oriented and are couched quantitatively in terms of output, time and improvement, e.g.:
  - 'Increase materials efficiency by three per cent before Quarter 3.'
  - 'Reduce invoice errors to less than five per month before July.'
- about behavioural improvement such as interpersonal skills, teamwork, open behaviour, leadership, etc., e.g.:
  - 'Set up team meetings to agree and progress improvement goals.'
  - 'Improve relationships with Tom, Dick, Harry and Mary by more open communication, involvement and casual recognition.'
- related to skills improvement such as job knowledge, planning, communication, IT skills, etc., e.g.:
  - 'Learn the operation of section C to a standard to take full control in Quarter 2.'
  - 'Complete training in statistical techniques and achieve one successful application by September.'
  - 'Become a proficient user of the approved spreadsheet software within Quarter 1.'

AGREED OBJECTIVES 1

A
| Name |
| Review Period |
| Supervisor's Name |

B

Agreed Objectives for Review Period and Subsequent Amendments
1. To appraise, coach, counsel and develop staff to help them improve their own performance throughout the year

FIGURE 10.14   Appraisal form – objectives
Source: BP Chemicals

Step 2
Communication is entered into about the process, its purpose, its administration, time scale and who is involved.

Step 3
Employees assess their own achievements and shortcomings, their results against targets and how and what they have improved. They will also comment on any training received and any skills developed as a result and how those skills have been applied. Finally they will estimate their own performance rating.

Step 4
Upward feedback. The employees comment on how the line manager has helped or hindered the performance described in Step 3. They indicate areas of behaviour or style that could be changed with advantage.

Step 5
The appraisal form (Fig 10.15, pages 143-144) is returned to the line manager who drafts some initial comments. A draft of a behaviours and skills profile will also be drawn up against a prescribed check list (Fig. 10.16, pages 145-146). At this point the manager will also consult with colleagues about the performance, interaction and relationships with other departments or teams.

Step 6
The line manager will set a date for the interview being careful to allocate adequate time.

Step 7
The interview. This should be as relaxed as possible and held in a conversational style while addressing the subject matter in a formal and systematic way. The employee's comments will be discussed and set against the line manager's views. The behavioural and skills profile will be discussed and a position under each heading is agreed. An overall

performance rating is agreed if possible; where agreement is not possible (rare), then the line manager's view prevails.

Step 8
An action plan is drawn up and will refer to such issues as:
- ongoing targets, objectives and milestones
- job content changes
- learning objectives and training
- increased responsibility
- increased exposure, etc.

Step 9
The employee has the opportunity to make and record any additional comments as a result of the interview.

Step 10
The appraisal form is signed together by the employee and the line manager.

Step 11
The next line managers (grandparents) review the forms for consistency of standards both of the comments and the ratings. They may unusually suggest a change of rating or wish to add a note of their own; in these cases they must communicate and explain the changes to the employees concerned.

Purpose
Formally recorded, the appraisal forms the basis for adjudging performance-related pay and bonuses. It should present a rounded picture of these features:
- performance against objectives (results)
- skills
- behaviour
- team performance
- improvement.

● MEASURES OF PERFORMANCE

PERFORMANCE REVIEW 2

A

Name
Registered No./Employee No.
Review Period
Supervisor's Name

B

Your own performance: How do you assess it against the objectives set?

C

How has your supervisor helped and how could he/she assist you further?

Contd.

FIGURE 10.15 Appraisal form – performance (contd.)
Source: BP Chemicals

D

Supervisor's Comments and Agreed Actions

E

Rating	Outstanding Performance (O)		Superior Performance (S)	
	Effective Performance (E)		Under Performance (U)	

F

Any other comments you wish to make

G

Signature	Supervisor's Signature	Date
Next Line Manager's Signature		

FIGURE 10.15 (contd.)

● MEASURES OF PERFORMANCE

ESSENTIAL BEHAVIOURS 'CHECKLIST' 2A

| Name |
| Review Period |

Definition	Supervisor's Comments	Assessment (tick scale) Strong ◄──► Weak
Open thinking Radical thinker, challenges old ideas and traditional thinking. Can see connections and patterns that others do not. Quickly identifies key issues in complex problems. Open to others' original ideas.		
Bias for action Looks to the future, and seeks opportunities and new ideas. Undaunted by risks and difficulty. Anticipates problems and uses many sources in order to clarify and solve them.		
Knows what makes others tick Takes time to understand people, gets to know their standpoint, their needs and concerns. Knows how to motivate. Encourages others to talk and express themselves.		
Concern for impact Considers impact of action on others, builds respect and trust for actions. Changes behaviour to suit the situation.		
Self-confidence Confident of ability, will take on challenge and accept responsibility for success or failure. Willing to evaluate own role and behaviour.		
Coaching and developing Accepts responsibility and encourages commitment to developing others. Sets realistic contracts, gives clear feedback, monitors progress, provides support.		
Building team success Makes clear contribution to the team. Encourages joint decisions and problem solving. Anticipates and resolves conflict and gives clear roles.		
Motivating Uses individuals' strengths. Knows what motivates individuals and uses this to get the best out of people. Varies style and mode of encouragement.		
Influencing others Unafraid of expressing negative opinions but emphasizes common interests and uses other people where necessary to add further weight.		

Contd.

FIGURE 10.16 Appraisal form – behaviours (contd.)
Source: BP Chemicals

MOTIVATING YOUR ORGANIZATION

ESSENTIAL BEHAVIOURS 'CHECKLIST' 2A

Name

Review Period

Definition	Supervisor's Comments	Assessment (tick scale) Strong ◄──────► Weak
Open thinking Radical thinker, challenges old ideas and traditional thinking. Can see connections and patterns that others do not. Quickly identifies key issues in complex problems. Open to others' original ideas.		
Bias for action Looks to the future, and seeks opportunities and new ideas. Undaunted by risks and difficulty. Anticipates problems and uses many sources in order to clarify and solve them.		
Knows what makes others tick Takes time to understand people, gets to know their standpoint, their needs and concerns. Knows how to motivate. Encourages others to talk and express themselves.		
Concern for impact Considers impact of action on others, builds respect and trust for actions. Changes behaviour to suit the situation.		
Self-confidence Confident of ability, will take on challenge and accept responsibility for success or failure. Willing to evaluate own role and behaviour.		
Coaching and developing Accepts responsibility and encourages commitment to developing others. Sets realistic contracts, gives clear feedback, monitors progress, provides support.		
Building team success Makes clear contribution to the team. Encourages joint decisions and problem solving. Anticipates and resolves conflict and gives clear roles.		
Motivating Uses individuals' strengths. Knows what motivates individuals and uses this to get the best out of people. Varies style and mode of encouragement.		
Influencing others Unafraid of expressing negative opinions but emphasizes common interests and uses other people where necessary to add further weight.		

Contd.

FIGURE 10.16 (contd.)

It also provides a data base from which to plan future improvements and training.

Appraisal must be an open process to the employee at all stages – there must be no secret part of the form where things are written that are not revealed.

Potential and career development

The appraisal is also a source of data to identify the potential of employees and to guide their career development. In fact in many systems the appraisal interview includes a strong element of this. At some point the conversation changes from performance review and action planning into career counselling. Some companies have found advantage in separating the two aspects. This method has several benefits in that it allows:
- time for more mature thought about career paths and realistic possibilities
- employees to take more responsibility for their own career planning
- other professionals and managers to become involved
- mature reflection on the results of the performance reviews and subsequent discussions with colleagues
- the performance review to concentrate on performance.

Performance ratings

Most appraisal systems have a form of rating – 1, 2, 3, 4 or, as in the BP example, O, S, E and U:

O Outstanding
S Superior
E Effective
U Underperforming

Some systems go for five categories, as with the Nissan example:

Outstanding
Highly commended
Fully proficient
Below expected performance
Unsatisfactory

In all cases, all employees are expected to be placed in the top three ratings. Ratings give a clear way of linking performance with pay. They inject a degree of objectivity that facilitates communication. There are some disadvantages:

- They assume an average performance as being effective E or acceptable 3 with the 'reward generating' performances being O and S or 1 and 2. Because 80 per cent of employees fall into E or 3 there is pressure to corrupt the ratings, to create sub-categories of E+ or 3+.
- The appraisal interview can degenerate into a haggle over ratings and to lose genuine messages about performance and behaviour.
- Management tend to look only at the ratings rather than read the comments.

A pilot study at one site in 'no ratings' appraisal found a majority of those taking part to be in favour, believing that the improved focus of the appraisal interview outweighed worries concerning subjectivity in calculating PRP. However, it is difficult to see how one can escape some form of evaluation of performance in order to make the connection with income improvement. The key test is whether the recipients understand that their pay has improved by x per cent as a result of their performance characterized in the appraisal process.

BASIC RULES OF PERFORMANCE MEASUREMENT

There are some basic rules to be followed when measuring performances:
1. Concentrate on the key issues – do not succumb to analysis paralysis.
2. Avoid setting minimum standards – they will either always be met (as if by magic), or they will damage cultural progress.
3. Data must be analysed to convert it to information.
4. Measurement must be seen to lead to action (e.g. performance-related rewards).
5. Make no judgements about performance without measurement – manage by facts, not wishful thinking.
6. Let the measures fit the work and the workers – the best fit and the best ownership is achieved when the workers develop their own measures.

● MEASURES OF PERFORMANCE

7 Create a sharing, learning environment in which comparison is acceptable.
8 Avoid Pitts' Law (see Chapter 8) – construct measures that are not vulnerable to manipulation.

Summary

1 Performance measures not rate-of-work measures.
2 Understand the process model.
3 The progress of the TQ process
   - assessment – against EQA or MBNQA criteria; benchmarking
   - self-assessment – ongoing, economic, ownership.
4 Outputs
   - EFQM model
   - stakeholders as a term for receivers of outputs
   - to shareholders, customers, employees and the community
   - financial results, customer satisfaction, employee surveys and other indicators, noise, effluent and emission loads, education links and press coverage.
5 Inputs
   - processes – essential requirements to complete a process and potential for improvement
   - key business processes
     - need to identify
     - analysis for opportunities for improvement
     - performance measurement links to strategic focus
     - examples: supply chain, innovation, customer management, people management, capital management
     - measuring improvement in lead times, cycle times, added value, cost reduction and environmental impact.
   - Process capability
     - a direct measure of improvement potential
     - if $C_p \leq 1$ there is room for improvement
     - six sigma quality can be a target.

- process control – measuring number of excursions beyond control limits over time
- quality assurance – compliance to procedures, measuring deficiencies at audit
- benchmarking – comparative measurement internally, with competitors or similar functions, yields gap between you and 'best in class'; the gap varies across a range of activities and can be represented in a comparative profile.

6 Metrics
  - essential characteristics
    - easily understood
    - readily comparable
    - adding value
    - strategically related
    - good ownership
    - incorruptible.
  - key performance indicators – defining the performance of key business processes; examples from the supply chain and customer satisfaction
  - experience curves – KPIs over time related to management initiatives provide lessons. What sort of improvement is needed? Continuous or step change?
  - defect measures – aligned with TQ, there is a disproportionate effect
  - Price of Non-conformance – Cost of Quality
  - comparisons – useful in an open learning culture.

7 Goal setting
  - vital to the performance improvement – measurement – reward system
  - links performance to performance of the company against its strategy
  - stretched goals have a place in motivating teams and businesses
  - essential features – agreed, owned team-related, relevant to key business processes, quantitative, timed, challenging, develop from success and learn from failure.

● MEASURES OF PERFORMANCE

8 Behaviour
   - absolutes
     - boundaries of acceptable behaviour
     - protect company reputation and endorse values.
   - essential behaviours defined
     - open thinking
     - personal impact
     - empowering
     - networking
     - assessment as an element of performance.
9 Other soft issues
10 Appraisal
   - formal systematic system
   - based on performance, skill development and deployment and behaviour – how as well as what
   - top-down with an element of bottom-up feedback
   - linked to, but separate from, career development
   - the place of performance ratings.
11 Basic rules of performance measurement.

CHAPTER 11

Leading on learning and nurturing knowledge

DYNAMIC SYSTEMS AND INTERACTION

Systems of work are interactive and cannot be regarded as stand-alone. One of the commonest causes of failure of TQ has been a failure to integrate it totally into all the working systems of an organization; too often it has been regarded as an interesting parallel activity to the real business of work or as only to be applied to certain aspects of the operation. Juran (1988) has said that management at the time was still not integrating continuous improvement into day-to-day work, strategy, budgets, planning and customer interaction. The reality is that any organization is not a collection of individual processes or even process chains but a complex system of interactions of those processes and, crucially, the people that operate them.

Chief executives and chairmen of organizations have been saying for years that people are their most important asset, without actually doing anything to show that they might understand what that meant. Their role in an organization is to lead on learning not on preaching and to demonstrate what they have learnt by changing the way that they do things themselves and the way that they expect others to do things.

The expediency of the reaction to short-term pressures, such as costs and restructuring, too often shows the fragility of what has been learnt about TQ thinking. Experience of the past rather than knowledge of the processes of change prompts reaction. Even in teams there can be a tendency for people to defend their own package of knowledge, to know what they know and to believe that they need know no more – what Peter Senge (1992) calls 'skilled incompetence'. Senge argues that the enduring organizations of the future will be 'learning organizations'. He defines five disciplines that will characterize this state of continuous learning. One of the five is systems thinking – events are not isolated but are inexorably linked within a system of interrelated actions and reactions. They are the consequences and initiators of a complex interlinked mesh of processes. To deal with them in isolation would be at best a misdirection of resources and at worst could be a complete misunderstanding of their significance.

Throughout this book I have emphasized the importance of process thinking and in particular the alignment of reward and recognition policy to the culture change process. It is an intimate part of the system that integrates total quality into the processes to satisfy customers and stakeholders. People are indeed the most important asset of an organization: without them it knows nothing, it does nothing, it carries out no processes, it changes nothing, it learns nothing. So policies that recognize the contribution of people to these systems are obligatory, not optional. Properly formulated and used, they can and should be an insistent reminder of the need for systems thinking.

CONTINUOUS LEARNING AND ESSENTIAL COMPETENCIES

Continuous learning is not a soft option. We must know what skills and competencies we need to develop by learning. The clever organizations will be able to fit their need for competency to the personal interests and ideals that are the natural inclinations of its staff; and vice versa they will recruit those with the appropriate aspirations in place. Vital encouragement and guidance will be given by rewarding and recognizing progress in the required skills. For example, a typical set of required competencies may be:

1. *Open behaviours*: a role model for those behaviours that we have referred to previously (see Chapter 10).
2. *Teamwork*: the ability to work in, set up and lead teams.
3. *Change management*: an understanding of the strategic value of change, the ability to initiate the process and to understand the steps and create a learning environment.
4. *Performance improvement*: an ability to define goals and performance indicators, to identify opportunities for improvement by process analysis and active listening, to facilitate implementation through coaching, empowering, motivation, reward and recognition.
5. *Innovation*: an aptitude to recognize opportunities, take considered risks, and act beyond experience.
6. *Customer focus*: customer satisfaction is the priority driver, a focus to anticipate customer needs and act on them, a knowledge and understanding of the market place.
7. *Professional and technical skill*: highly developed expertise, a guardian of the knowledge asset base.
8. *Cultural alignment*: focusing on the long term, a concern for 'how' as well as 'what', communication at all stages and the integration of activities of functions and processes with strategic goals, the practice of systems thinking.

SOME PRACTICAL ASPECTS OF CONTINUOUS LEARNING

Those companies that embrace continuous learning are expanding their training activities by orders of magnitude in terms of man-hours and money. Large organizations begin to resemble universities in that formal training is a constant element of work at all levels. Motorola spends one per cent of its sales turnover on training and IBM expects its managers to spend at least 40 hours per year in off-the-job training.

The officially sponsored UK initiative called 'Investors in People' (see also Chapter 10) provides an opportunity for any organization, irrespective

of size, to compare its investment in the training and development of its people against a national standard. The standard has elements relating to:
- commitment from top managers to develop employees to achieve business objectives
- planning – training is regularly reviewed and plans for the needs of all employees are prepared
- action to train and develop employees throughout their employment
- evaluation of the investment in training and development to assess achievement and improve future effectiveness.

It is early days to assess the impact of this initiative. I suspect its ultimate success will depend upon the extent to which the standard requires continuous learning at all levels of an organization and the involvement of employees in formulating their own learning plans.

Classroom training is only part of the story; it is equally about creating an environment in which the whole work experience is about learning, where innovation and risk-taking are encouraged and failure is seen as a source of learning rather than a case for penalty. Where, to encourage the innovative spirit, we might even reward and recognize a failed initiative because of its learning value.

More and more of our learning will be on-the-job and the skills of managers and team leaders as coaches and facilitators will be an increasingly important aspect of performance for reward.

BOFFINS ARE BEAUTIFUL, SPECIALISTS ARE SPECIAL

In deploying reward and recognition policies within learning organizations there is an obligation to reinforce the status of those who are the depository of the knowledge asset of the organization. There are non-human ways of storing knowledge in data bases and expert systems, but these are wedges that capture our state of knowledge as it moves up the hill of learning driven by the energy of creativity (see Fig. 11.1). This is the same function that systems perform in the process of improvement (see Fig. 11.2). It is the boffin on whom we depend to supply the energy for the development of that asset. The inhibitions of the old hierarchies should have collapsed in the

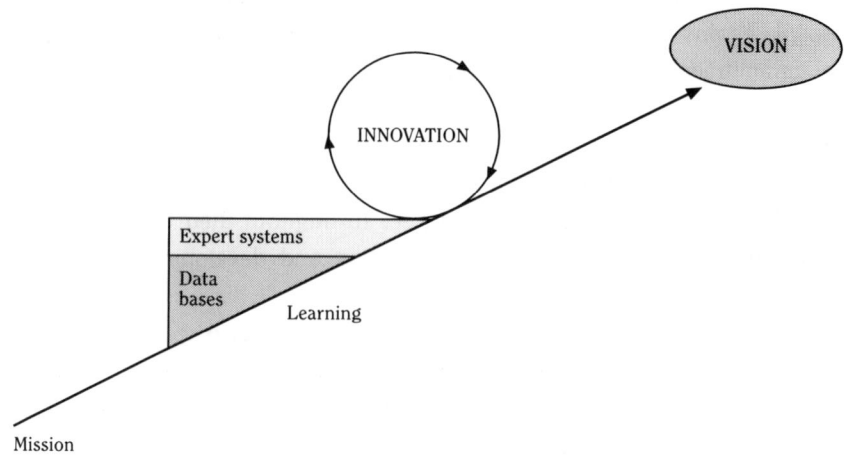

FIGURE 11.1 The learning hill

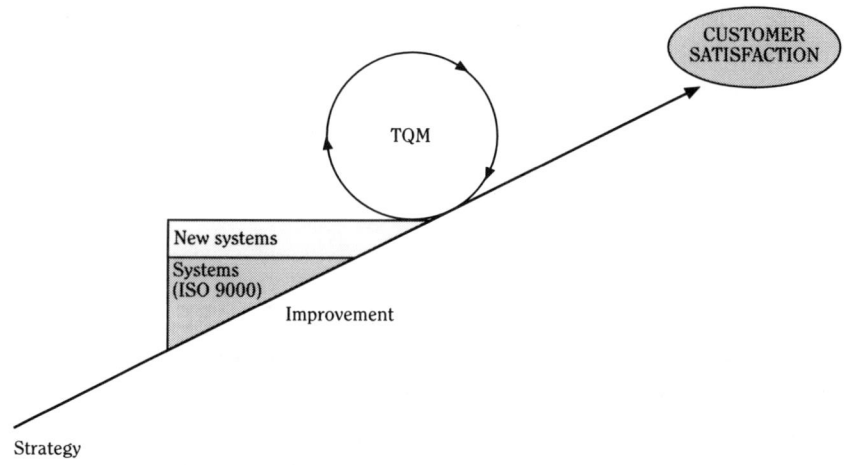

FIGURE 11.2 The improvement hill

flatter organizations of today. No longer can it be justified to regard specialists as long-haired boffins who could not be advanced up the managerial ladder and therefore became prematurely stalled in terms of reward. There can be no more culturally correct candidates for reward and recognition than those whose achievement is in the development of the key knowledge assets, in innovation, creative thinking and the inventive application of specialist skills. The rate at which these processes can be carried out will be crucial to the success of tomorrow's companies. The power of reward and recognition must be used in support of this aim.

Eccentrics

In a learning organization we should strive to push out the boundaries of our conventional knowledge and expose the possibilities beyond. Henry Mintzberg, the unconventional Canadian writer on management, suggests that business success does not flow automatically from an MBA: 'To be superbly successful you have to be a visionary – someone with a very novel vision of the world...' (Mintzberg, 1993). It is the unconventional thinkers, the radicals, those that are impatient for change, those who threaten the status quo who are the vehicles for discovery. Rather than regarding them as a nuisance who take up too much management time, they should be encouraged, rewarded and recognized.

REWARDING SKILL

In Chapter 7 the concept of skill-based pay was discussed and in particular the extension of skills into multi-skilling and the enriching of the job. Employees are being asked to learn all but the most specialist skills in order to do a complete task and, importantly, to take responsibility for it, to be accountable for QA, for production time, for costs and, of course, for improvement. Production operations are being organized in 'cells' in which a complete operation is carried out and the team within that cell is responsible for it. Members of the team will learn each job within the cell to achieve maximum flexibility. Even production line operations such as car assembly are being organized in this fashion, with each shop or section being set up in this flexible multi-skilled team approach. In the learning organization of the future, rather than this being a top-down imposition, it will be a bottom-up, demand-led natural requirement of whole-job commitment, accountability and satisfaction. The chemical plant operator will expect not only to be able to operate all pieces of equipment on his plant, but also to be able to carry out simple maintenance and repair tasks too.

To take another example from the chemicals sector: because of the safety implications of chemical plant operations it is necessary to ensure that certain actions are carried out in a definite sequence; the operations often go on across several shifts as well, so to achieve adequate control it is necessary to signify in writing when each activity is complete. For years the trade union prevented its members signing anything – their members were not paid to take responsibility, that was management's role. In future the multi-skilled, whole-job operators will be proud to take responsibility and to sign their work.

Multi-skilling is a manifestation of the need to learn continuously, and job enrichment is a step on the way to the environment of the true learning organization.

LEADING ON LEARNING

At the start of this chapter I said that the role of chairmen and CEOs was to lead on learning. In 1990 Peter Senge looked forward to the restructuring of management development to focus on the roles, skills and tools for leadership in learning organizations (Senge, 1990). He also exhorted his readers to begin seriously to explore this territory in order to realize a vision of leadership that commanded respect through credibility and empowerment. Today's leaders have to accept that they must be role models of learning and must enable empowerment through coaching and facilitation.

CONCLUDING REMARKS

To summarize this short chapter on the importance of learning organizations and nurturing knowledge and their relationship with reward and recognition, I would first address those sceptics who believe that this is all common sense and a statement of the obvious. If you believe that, I would ask you to step out into the real world of work and try to introduce even the most modest change and note the reaction. All the old barriers are still there; the concept of learning from others and sharing best practice is dogged by 'not invented here'. The idea of performance-related pay is dismissed as unfair, divisive or impossible to measure. The concepts of empowerment are said to be too risky in some industries. And the concept of continuous learning is rejected in favour of the tried and tested methods.

I believe strongly that our attitudes in life are forged in the fire of experience, the most formative being emotional, and therefore to change attitudes requires us to work at the emotional level. This explains why people accept change more readily and more rapidly when confronted with some perceived fear or crisis. Therefore in our most formative years, when emotions are most active in all aspects of life, we should be exposed to the concept of continuous learning. Let us not give young people the idea that learning is for school and college and stops when they start work.

Our entrenched views of work and how we relate to it, what Peter Senge calls our mental models, are resistant to change but change they must. Our mental model of the organization we work in has to change from that comfortable command-and-control hierarchy to the risky open, empowered, learning environment. Our mental model of our competencies has to change. Our mental model of reward and recognition has to change too. Because this last one operates more naturally at an emotional level it can help to catalyse if not lead change in the other models.

Reward and recognition at all levels should be instrumental in encouraging the key attributes required in a learning organization: an awareness of and willingness to change mental models, systems thinking, shared visions, a willingness to learn, open communication, teams and teamworking. If all of this has the ring of familiarity about it with the themes that I have advanced in earlier chapters then I am glad, because I believe it stands repetition.

CHAPTER 12

The future

It is playing a fool's game for those who believe in continuous change to try to predict the future, because at any point in time they are unlikely to be right and if they were right they would not be satisfied. My excuse for doing so is that it may serve to clarify at least the direction in which we are being taken by the ideas put forward earlier in this book.

Human beings have an inexorable capacity to adapt to their environment and this will come into play. There will be many who are stimulated by being able to set their own rules for achievement. More of us are likely to work for three or four different employers in our normal working lives, thus it will become crucial to construct a portfolio of attainment as we pass through each one. The motivating effect of such a regime seems to be more direct and, for the young and eager, more satisfying.

I have seen early signs of this at work. A young man – let us call him Jack – joined the junior management in a position where he could gain experience for two or three years. The real responsibility for running the plant rested with a more senior man who had been in post for about four years. He, in turn, reported to a more senior man who had responsibility for this and another similar plant and he, in his turn, reported to a more senior manager who looked after a group of plants. The plants were actually run by operators who reported to a shift supervisor. Jack was a bright young man who enjoyed everything he did or else he did not want to do it. He was keen to learn and so learned quickly; in six months he had mastered the essential technical understanding of the process and had tried his hand at some minor management tasks. He was doing very well. At a routine interview, I looked forward to telling him that he had made a promising start and could anticipate a rewarding future. However, Jack did not let me enjoy that moment; he pre-empted the conversation by telling me that he was bored. When could he do something that would really challenge him? It took a major benchmarking exercise to tell us that we had an outdated management structure in our plant area, which prompted us to remove layers and gave Jack his opportunity. He now manages the plant single-handed with just a team of shift supervisors to help him. He has his challenge and is enjoying it. The value added is that he is getting to grips with longstanding problems which for months or years previously had gone up and down the hierarchical maze. To achieve this he is having to use all the latest tricks of the trade, all the tools and techniques of TQ and teamwork. But he is being effective, he has his team, they are empowered, they have their goals and are going for them. This will be one model of the future.

THE TOTAL QUALITY CONTINUUM

There are those who say that total quality has had its day – yes, it played a part in the 1980s in defining quality and pointing us in the direction of the customer, but it will not be enough for sustained success in the 1990s. One can read many a paper headed 'Beyond Total Quality'. To hold this sort of view is to play the consultancy fad game; it places TQ into too narrow a confine and devalues what has been achieved. Much of the problem has been a concentration on technique while principles became confused. In May 1993 the *Wall Street Journal* carried a report (Naj, 1993) about US manufacturers who were abandoning some of the techniques they had imported from Japan because they had not delivered the expected benefits; but to try to bolt on quality circles here or *kanban* there and JIT (just-in-time) somewhere else without looking at the whole system and the key processes is doomed to failure. How often has one met anxious managers wondering whether they should install quality circles when they have perfectly good existing work groups just waiting to be empowered to get on with improvement? If the principles are understood and there is a realization that there is no such thing as *the* quality process but only the quality process that suits the particular organization, tailored to its needs and not a slavish copy of a few high-profile techniques, then more people will enjoy the benefits of TQM far into the future.

If total quality is defined as *continuously improving the efficiency and effectiveness of our processes to satisfy our stakeholders*, then I think that it quite rightly embraces much of recent thinking – certainly process thinking, systems thinking, continuous learning and 'investing in people'. Even apparently discontinuous step-changes such as re-engineering can be seen as a necessary part of the improvement continuum. We have seen (Chapter 10) that benchmarking can reveal the gap between one's own position and the 'best in class', and that continuous improvement alone would not be enough to achieve competitiveness but, on the other hand, step-changes alone would be insufficient to sustain the position.

And so all of these things move us up the improvement curve (Fig. 12.1) and, if we are always deploying some of them, improvement will be more or less continuous. We will be continuously improving our processes to satisfy the stakeholders and if the customer is not satisfied then the

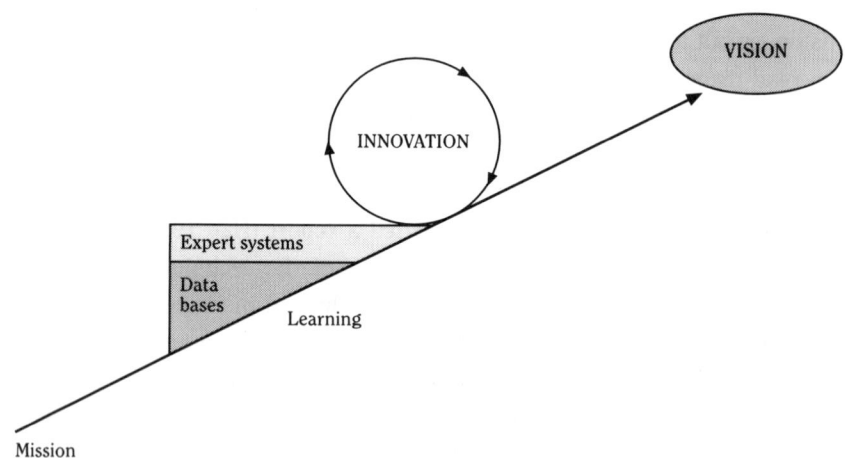

FIGURE 12.1 Performance improvement node

● THE FUTURE

other stakeholders cannot be. For me this is total quality. Of course, although it is continuous it is not constant – we must be prepared to alter our approach whenever we detect a node on the effects-effort curve (Fig 12.2). Failure to do this or to place the new initiative firmly within the TQ continuous improvement continuum will not only discredit what has gone before but make it much harder to generate motivation for the new approach. Conversely, if it is seen as a natural and necessary extension to the TQ process, then it can be introduced with optimum effect at the appropriate point when current efforts are running out of steam.

The academic and consulting community has an important role in clarifying all of this. There is a worrying tendency for too many organizations to jump on a bandwagon of phraseology, to grasp the latest slickly marketed piece of jargon, without understanding the principles or the significance with respect to what has gone before. James Champy, who co-authored with Michael Hammer a definitive book on re-engineering (Hammer and Champy, 1993), was recently reported as being concerned that the term 're-engineering' had become too generic and organizations were flattering their downsizing activities with it without really understanding, much less applying, the principles (Mullin, 1993).

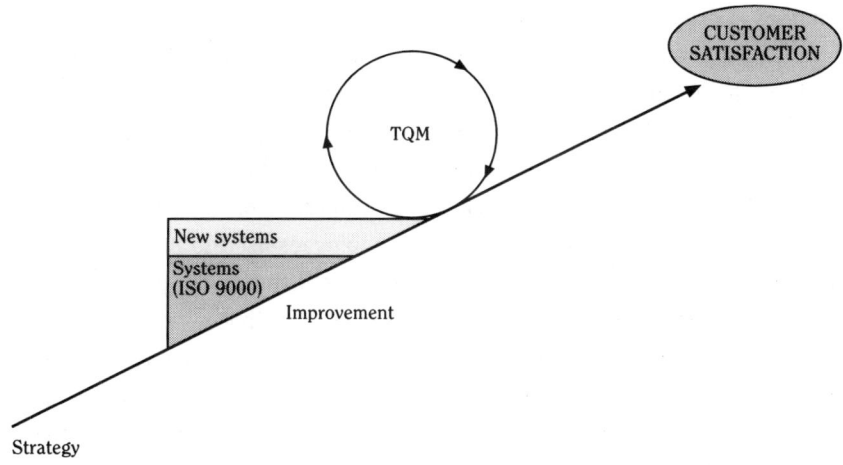

FIGURE 12.2 Continuous not constant

THE PLACE FOR REWARD AND RECOGNITION

Reward and recognition must be part of this continuum, not divorced from it. A sure recipe for failure is to introduce new reward systems or PRP in isolation and before the culture has changed to a point where they can be accepted.

Reward and recognition will never become ends in themselves but will remain important supporting processes vital to the effective and efficient progress of those key processes on which businesses and enterprises depend. I have stressed in several passages in the book the importance of alignment of reward and recognition policies with the desired culture. Non-alignment will actually prevent development of the culture and can initiate its decline.

As regards the future I would go further, and insist that these policies must not merely align but must assimilate. They must be an integral part of the cultural fabric; personnel departments must not operate in parallel with the planners and strategic thinkers but must be part of that process. Too often one has seen them following, desperately trying to formulate policies that are appropriate to the strategic development, the cultural shifts, after they have appreciated what they are. Reward and recognition must be part of the debate from the outset, they must be transparently part of the changes – drivers not consequences.

There is a real possibility that there will be more than lip service paid to the cliché that people are an organization's most precious asset. Considerations of reward and recognition put people in the frame automatically, especially as in future we will be paying the person not the job. Reward systems will recognize the contributions of real people, not the output of productive units or 'hands', as employees used to be called at the time of the industrial revolution and indeed until the recent past. This will be done not as an act of faith but because we want that contribution from that particular person, not just a task completed. We will have exposed and reversed the 'hidden assumption' (Chapter 3) because we know we want everyone's heads as well as their hands. Chapter 1 described the privilege that some of us had enjoyed in being able to satisfy our need for achievement in our working lives; this privilege will be the common experience rather than the exception and will be fertilized by reward and recognition.

THE FRUITS OF REWARD

If reward is to take the place that I am suggesting it should, we must give people the time and space to enjoy the fruits of that reward. Otherwise, however cleverly we design the reward package, the motivational edge will be dulled if it cannot facilitate a fulfilling life outside work. Those very people in whom we have released the drive to contribute in full at work will also wish to contribute to, and enjoy, non-work areas too. 'All work and no play makes Jack a dull boy' goes the old saying, and in future Jack will not be prepared to be a dull boy. So improved reward and recognition will bring increased motivation, even dedication, but cannot assume unlimited energy, concentration or time.

In the days when work was just a place to spend 44 hours each week and not something that one did and thought about, there were at least 60 or 70 hours a week to live a life outside work. The balance has gone too far in the other direction and will be corrected. It is unreasonable for any employee, whatever he or she is paid, or however important he or she may be, to have to spend 70 hours a week actually engaged in work and a further 20 or 30 thinking about it. It represents a style that accords status to indispensability (real or imagined), gains credibility by the length of time at the desk, gives recognition for the acceptance of impossible targets, and sets its only measure as success or winning. The associated problems of managing failure and being a loser do not seem to deter the devotees of this approach.

Even those who subscribe to this style of pseudo-dedication do actually have covert private agendas – to buy a yacht, to set up on their own at 40, to gain a partnership and then sit back – and so will be working to relatively short-term perspectives.

The popular thrust in the future will be to gauge success by contribution, that is, overall contribution both in and out of work; and there will be an expectation for the opportunity to achieve both.

FUTURE STRUCTURES

Small is beautiful

At the beginning of the 1980s I was fortunate enough to be sent to a factory that was out of the mainstream of my company's operation. At the time I did not realize that I had been accorded a privilege – indeed some of my colleagues offered sympathy about my being despatched to the 'sticks'. But I can say in all sincerity that I have never enjoyed work so much as I did in this assignment. The secret of my being so at ease was that the factory was small (150 people) and was allowed to operate independently, with no interference from the 'centre'. Nonetheless the Company sign hung proudly at the gate and those 150 souls were indeed proud to be part of that huge organization, and needed little encouragement to operate to standards that would never harm its reputation. In fact there were several occasions when this little backstreet factory enhanced the prestige of that Goliath both commercially, technically and by its community activities. It also provided a rich source of training for new graduate staff.

Without putting any fancy names to the process, we organized the supply chain horizontally, we formed multi-disciplined teams, began multi-skilling, introduced measurement, reduced inventories and customer response times and involved everybody in these processes. These things were not done without some difficulties but all of them were achieved with a degree of success within a few years. I now know why this was possible: the answer is we were beautifully small and we were empowered. With 150 people it is possible to know every one of them by their first names and to know something of their hopes and fears, their troubles and joys – in fact, to have a relationship with each of them. That makes it relatively easy to explain what change is about and their part in it. We took advantage of the trust that the 'centre' put in us to do our own thing, take our own risks, make our own mistakes, to lead on learning and nurture our own knowledge. In return we operated to high standards, kept the company flag flying locally and came to make sensible profits. When TQM came along in 1988 it was applied without difficulty; there already was customer focus, but continuous improvement and the continuous improvement cycle of plan-do-check-act were added with good effect.

As the years have passed and I have observed the rest of the organization struggle to achieve the culture change that seemed so natural in that little factory, I have understood the importance of size and in particular the importance of small size. Of course, now it is preaching to the converted. Tom Peters (1992) talks of 'necessary disorganisation' and quotes the examples of ABB (the Swedish/Swiss electrical and heavy machinery giant) reorganizing its 215 000 people into 50 person profit centres, of BTR (the UK conglomerate) and its 500 profit centres. He also gives examples from the same companies of decentralization: ABB has only 150 central staff, BTR has 47 and Richard Branson's Virgin Group only 5! We have seen this trend to decentralize translated into a spate of management buy-outs in the UK where conglomerates have sought to divest stand-alone units that were not essential to their core operations. In many cases where the local dedicated teams arranged to buy the business they have been very successful; Leyland Trucks, for example, turned a huge loss-making, bankrupt business into a £6 m profit within 11 months.

So the lesson I unwittingly learnt in the early 1980s is now common knowledge; in the future it looks set to become common practice. That is good news for reward and recognition because it means that it will be easier to identify teams, easier to delegate the application and easier to tailor the format to have local credibility.

However, the sense of belonging to a larger organization as well as a small 'team' should be jealously preserved to provide standards, a sense of wider purpose and a trusted source of assistance – what Charles Handy (1994) has called twin citizenship and subsidiarity. Reward and recognition properly applied can be an essential ingredient of the cement that holds the disorganized organization together.

Flat and empowered

As we stop commanding and controlling, and organizations de-layer and contract, hierarchies collapse and salary structures collapse with them. As we empower teams to implement their own actions to progress towards their own goals, there is no longer a need for 'middle managers' to interpret, communicate and control the application of the wishes of the senior management, therefore a complete cadre of professionals disappear. The death of the middle manager means often that three or four levels of status and salary scale are eliminated. I well remember being an impatient young professional on the first rung of middle management complaining to my boss that my elevation to the next rung was overdue. He replied that though I might well deserve to be grade 10, I would have to wait until there was a suitable grade 10 job vacant. In future the hierarchy will not be there to protect this sort of thinking; we really will have to pay the person, not the job. We will have to recognize what people achieve, not the position they hold.

There are dangers in empowerment as well: a large number of empowered teams may lose sight of the organizational objectives, may stray from the overall mission or neglect the corporate values and standards. Worse still, they may not appreciate or consider the impact of their actions on interrelated systems. So there *is* a role for management even in the flattest organization, and there *is* a role for the 'centre' (however small) in the disorganized organization. But it is easier to understand the holistic view, to do the systems thinking in a small organization – small is beautiful.

If the culture change that empowered, flatter organizations represent is to continue to progress, the reward and recognition policies must be in step, and here particularly they have an opportunity to lead.

The essential core and the necessary clothes

If organizations are to be flatter and smaller, what will be their shape? It has been suggested that trefoil structures will be adopted by more and more organizations, what Handy (1989) has called 'shamrock organizations'. One leaf of the shamrock will be the comparatively small number of people in which is embodied the essential knowledge of the company. In this elite core the motivations are likely to be similar to those in a conventional structure, except that the population will have been distilled to the high-achieving few and so personal satisfaction will feature strongly. The second leaf of the shamrock will contain contracted-out functions, or in the current parlance, 'outsourcing'. This has commonly happened with fringe activities such as catering, security and building maintenance but is beginning to be seen in more central activities such as accounting, IT, and even personnel. Clearly here motivation will be by achievement through customer satisfaction; the principles of TQ will be the key. The third leaf is a source of flexible manpower – in other words, a source of workers with the required skills who will work as and when required on a personal contracting basis. These workers will have several companies as potential employers; their prospects for employment and the reward that they are able to command will depend absolutely on their established reputation – a powerful motivator to perform.

If, then, the organization is going to reduce to its essential core, it has to be able to define what it is that is essential in these terms, what it is that differentiates it from the next organization. In most cases it will be concluded that it is the unique knowledge residing in the organization and the ability to develop that knowledge base through continuous learning that makes it different, that gives it a competitive edge. Thus those few special people who are the guardians of that knowledge will be the key core staff and it is they who will be rewarded and recognized to encourage continuous learning, long-term thinking and loyalty; job-hopping will not be culturally acceptable behaviour. At last the long-serving specialists will come into their own.

The two leaves of the trefoil that will clothe the central core will not define its personality, but they will help to express it. And although they will have their own goals and motivations, these will have to be aligned with the core's strategy and vision. Their customers' satisfaction, and hence their reward and recognition, will depend on that alignment and in particular on their contribution to these customers' continuous improvement.

Teams and teamworking

You will not have got this far in this book without understanding my enthusiasm for teams. Many far-sighted companies and service organizations are already getting good value and have developed into multi-disciplined and self-managed teams. Whatever the format, I believe that they will be a commanding feature of the structures we employ up to, and well beyond, the millennium. This is no accident, it is because the facets of human behaviour and interaction that allow good teams to be successful and cause poor teams to fail are the same as those that so often inhibit the development of the potential of the individual. Individuals will make a more complete and more fulfilling contribution within the right team than on their own. Teams are the vehicles in which continuous learning will best occur and a sense of shared vision can flourish.

It follows that the behaviours that fit well with teamworking and the skills to achieve in the team situation will be in demand, will be important candidates for recognition and will be the elements of performance that attract increasing reward. The competencies that differentiate a leader from a manager will command special attention.

Individuals in the future can expect their rewards in large measure to reflect their performance as part of a team or teams. This does not detract from their individual performance but merely puts it in context. In team sports, the exceptionally gifted individual only shines when playing in a top flight team.

Multi-skilling and whole job responsibility

For more than 30 years enlightened employers have seen job enrichment as a way of creating motivation and job satisfaction (see Chapters 1 and 11). This approach is being rediscovered today and will be an imperative in the future.

Multi-skilling is and will remain a basis for reward. One way of improving one's position on the pay scale will be to become proficient in new skills. In future, reward should be focused on the output of those skills as well as their acquisition, to recognize the whole job, its product and the way it has been produced. Not only will whole-job workers be responsible for carrying out the work, they will all carry a responsibility to improve the way it is done as well.

Behaviour

Cultural determinants: the defining dozen
The cultures that are sustainably successful in the future will share the following dozen characteristics; in them people will:
- learn continuously
- improve continuously
- use customer satisfaction as a driver
- form relationships
- build and use effective teams
- have a long-term focus
- have shared visions
- understand common objectives
- successfully apply developed skills
- understand the processes involved and their interaction
- enjoy their contribution
- register achievement.

Implied essentials
This defining dozen implies a necessary pattern of behaviour that, for instance, is called, in the case of BP, the essential behaviours. These patterns of behaviour nearly equate to what used to be called style, but the difference is that style may have been desirable but it was optional. To use BP's term, essential behaviours are just that – essential. This is not to say that we must all behave as automatons, cloned in the imaginations of management consultants. Individual style will continue to spice our working relationships but it will be a matter of the relative emphasis of the constituent facets of the essential behaviours.

The defining dozen characteristics feature teams, and it is the ability to participate in teams effectively that is a test of much that is essential in the behaviour of the future. Chapter 3 discussed the behaviour changes necessary to convert from old style manager to team leader, and many of these will be features of team membership too:

1 *Listening.* We all need to hear what others are saying, to give it due credence and be prepared to modify our own views and actions as a result.
2 *Encouragement.* We need to notice when a fellow member is having a hard time and, to use the wild goose analogy, to honk from behind (Chapter 3).
3 *Support.* There will always be conflict in teams; we must be prepared to support another's point of view to help to resolve conflict positively.
4 *Coaching.* Teams are a mixture of skills and aptitudes; continuous learning demands that we are able to help others develop their skills and acquire new ones.
5 *Delegation.* We must be prepared to let whoever is best suited, to do the job, however prestigious it may be.
6 *Recognition.* Mutual recognition and joint celebration of achievement are strong binding influences in a team; appreciation of peers is a strong motivator for individual members.

There are four more behavioural features that will be necessary to add to the list generated by the team test:

1 *'Systems thinking'.* I interpret the term used by Senge (1992) as an understanding of the processes that they operate and their interaction with the complex mesh of processes that make up any business or service organization.
2 *Creative action.* The willingness to risk to innovate, to fail in order to learn, to remove barriers.
3 *Contextual understanding.* To see one's work in the overall picture, one's goals as part of the corporate vision, short-term objectives as milestones in the long-term strategy, and personal achievement through team and corporate success.
4 *Communication.* This is a word needing rejuvenation after much overuse, but if we are to share visions, strategies and goals, understand customers' needs, support our colleagues' aspirations and deliver on the defining dozen, then open, honest, uncompetitive, unprejudiced-communication at and across all levels is indeed essential.

Recognition and behaviour

In terms of achieving and demonstrating the desired behaviours, recognition is easy, highly geared and good value for money. I am not going to reiterate what was said in Chapters 4 and 5 but the increased application of these techniques will be perhaps the least dramatic and most telling change to the work culture of the millennium.

Reward and behaviour

The important point for the future is that behaviour will be measured and judged as part of performance, and that part will increase. Rewards for improvement in performance will include considerations of improvement in behaviour. Achievement will be seen to be a mix of 'What' and 'How'.

The semaphore of recognition and reward

The giving of recognition and reward will be seen as one of the ways an organization sends messages to its members: for example, if we recognize our 'best' people by giving them a bonus every year and promoting them every two years, we will be seen to be concerned with action rather than consequence, short-term results rather than long-term performance. Similarly, if annual increases are based on one year's results, then the recipients will understand that corporate thinking is limited to this short-term horizon. Publicly quoted companies have often suffered from the perceived need to deliver short-term performance for the shareholder; in future the other stakeholders' interests should exert their appropriate influence which, in turn, should lengthen board-room perspectives. Those parts of the reward package linked to corporate performance should reflect its performance against its long-term strategic plan rather than the snapshot financial measures.

The application of recognition and reward will have to signal that the essential behaviours are the only behaviours that attract commendation, whether they be the encouragement of sustainable long-term thinking or excellent teamwork or the learning and application of new skills. Meritorious behaviour will be that which contributes to the satisfaction of the stakeholders. Equally, behaviour that reduces the stakeholders' satisfaction will not be recognized or rewarded.

OWNERSHIP AND MEMBERSHIP

Ownership

In many places in this book I have promoted the concept of ownership because it smooths the path of change. If we believe that the changes are what we want we are more likely to put our energies into securing them. Ownership can be achieved by involving people in the process of change, by allowing them to participate in its development, and, most importantly, by telling them about it – what, why, when and how – and actively listening to their responses. This is not new and is practised widely in more and more organizations except, I contend, when it comes to changes in personnel policies, including reward and recognition. For some reason these are conceived, gestate, and are born within the secret rooms of personnel (HR) departments under the all-justifying cloak of 'confidentiality'. Small wonder, then, that when they are revealed they are often met with resistance, resentment and even fear. Reward and recognition policies must be part of the change process, and in some cases and at some times must lead it, and like any other change we must be involved, all of us, in the process. After all, we are stakeholders, our requirements must be determined and the means of satisfaction must be developed.

Membership

Organizations that embrace continuous change, continuous learning and continuous improvement have to genuinely include everyone within those organizations in those changes. They are members of the organization and, as Handy (1994) observes, ' ... [we] cease to be instruments or employees and become enfranchised.' In other words, we will enjoy membership in the true sense of the word, as if members of a club. This implies that policies such as reward and recognition must be completely open – there can be no suggestion of secrecy. What is more, the policies must find wide acceptability; when people are members they have a say in formulating and changing the rules. In good clubs there is a common understanding of its purpose, rules and strategy by all the members. That transparent understanding and accepted credibility will be present in the lastingly successful organizations of the 1990s and beyond.

Using the 'wheel on the hill' analogy again (Fig 12.3), motivation is the driving force up the 'membership hill' towards people satisfaction. If it is not to stop or regress, the supporting wedge of recognition and reward must be in place. What is more, we have to find a way of moving the wedge up the hill as well; in other words, reward and recognition have to be subject to continuous change too.

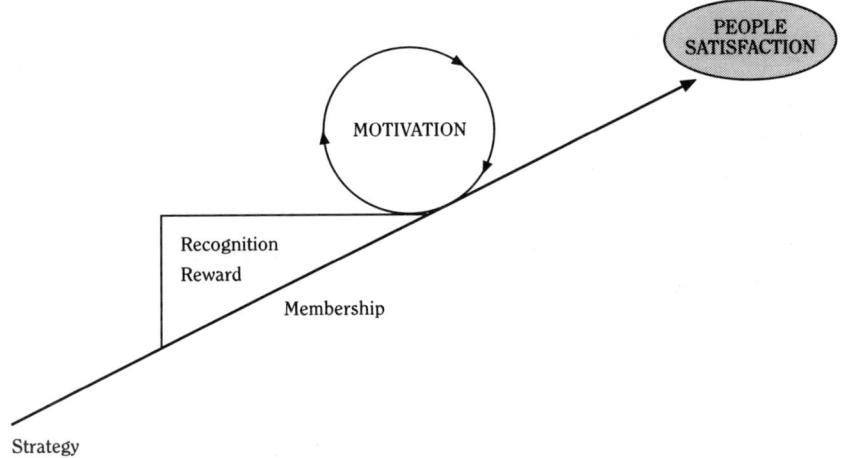

FIGURE 12.3 The membership hill

THE REWARD PACKAGE OF THE FUTURE

Chapter 9 set out the constituent features of a good reward package. I have also said that reward, like everything else will be subject to continuous change. Hopefully the direction of that change will be towards:
- Rewarding the person not the job.

- Rewarding how as well as what.
- Rewarding performance of the team, the individual within the team and the team as a part of the organization, all measured as improvement.
- Acceptable measures of performance for service organizations and professions.
- Performance defined as improvement in stakeholder satisfaction led by customer satisfaction, learning, innovation and creativity, and behaviour.
- A pay structure that has elements of
  - basic pay to set the context of relative worth
  - skill-based pay to recognize the acquisition, development and *application* of the necessary skills
  - performance-related pay with performance defined as above and agreed at appraisal; PRP will be committed and distributed on the principles of gainsharing
  - success sharing through *universal* share schemes and share options. Skill-based pay and PRP will become relatively larger as a proportion of total income.
- Local determination in small, decentralized, empowered profit centres.
- Openness and involvement of all in policy development.
- Seamless and coincident alignment with the changes resulting from the total quality process.

IT IS ALL ABOUT RECOGNITION

From the outset I have argued that there exists in all of us a need to be recognized and that that recognition is required to maintain motivation. The discussion surrounding reward and, in particular, performance-related reward suggests that reward is a form of recognition. As such we can use our obligation to pay employees to tell them that we are not just paying them for doing the job but that we appreciate the way that they have done it, the thought that they have brought to it, the skills that they have learned and deployed on it, the way in which they have worked with and related to others, and the improvements that they have achieved. All this will create a feeling of confidence, of being in tune with the cultural thrust of the organization, a feeling of belonging – membership. In that sort of environment people will continue to do good work, to be motivated.

Recognition is the demonstration by human beings that they have noticed and appreciated the actions, achievements and contribution of others. It is fundamental to humans being at ease with themselves, because it is thus that our very purpose is characterized, worthy or unworthy. Even the saints who shunned public acclaim were motivated by thought of divine recognition.

In a world that is flirting with the siren sounds and the wishful whirlpools of the acquisitive society, I hope that the power of recognition will be deployed, especially in the workplace, to guide our actions away from short-term financial and material success and towards longer-term visions of satisfaction – satisfaction for all of the stakeholders in an enterprise, spearheaded by the customer (the receiver of the outputs), without whom every other stake becomes worthless. We may indeed be driven by our own personal needs, but, given the right culture and the opportunity, we will also reveal our needs to be recognized as contributing to a bigger cause.

Final thought

This book has been about how we recognize and reward those who work in paid employment. There are those, however, who will find the subtleties of reward systems and performance-related pay of little interest or perhaps see them only as a sick joke and yet they have the same needs to make a contribution, to register achievement and to receive recognition. These are a significant group of people – they are the unemployed.

For the last 150 years unemployment in the UK has averaged around five per cent with excursions to over twenty per cent in the 1930s and to nearly zero in the 1940s. All the developments that we talk about in terms of improvement, efficiency, effectiveness, and IT often imply employing less people, and we are also getting better at learning so that we do not replace those who have been displaced under the pressure of recession. Thus the only apparent hope of significant reductions in unemployment is to expand the economy and create new employing businesses. The conclusion is that the future seems to hold prospects of unemployment for at least four per cent, which may sound acceptable until you translate that into actual people (two to three million in the UK alone) and this pattern is common to all of the developed free-enterprise economies. New patterns of employment, new organizational structures, and earlier retirement will all cloud the picture. In forming those patterns and structures we must be alive to the need to create new employing opportunities.

Clearly society has an obligation to use its ingenuity to create the opportunity to allow those people to register achievement, to make a contribution and to be recognized. Equally, those who are in paid employment have an obligation to ensure that the organizations to which they belong are following a cultural path which has the best chance of assuring long-term sustainable growth and health.

The principles of total quality and aligned reward and recognition will be an important instrument in the search for successful, maintainable, and meaningful employment in the coming decades.

References

Armstrong, M. (1993). *Managing Reward Systems*. Buckingham: Open University Press

BSI (1987). *BS 5750. Parts 1, 2 and 3*. London: British Standards Institute

BSI (1994). *BS EN ISO 9000, 1,2,3,4*. London: British Standards Institute

Camp, R.C. (1989). *Benchmarking, the Search for Industry Best Practices that Lead to Superior Performance*. Wisconsin: ASQC Quality Press

CBI (1980). London: Confederation of British Industry

Chemical Engineer (1993). Editorial, November

Corby, S. (1994). 'Corporate Britain's language of deceit'. *The Observer*, 12 June

Creelman, J. (1992). 'Commentary – Money Talks'. *TQM Magazine*, October, p. 267

Crosby, P.B. (1979). *Quality is Free*. New York: McGraw-Hill

Dale, B. and Cooper, C. (1992). *Total Quality and Human Resources*. Oxford: Blackwell Business Publications

Deming, W.E. (1982). *Out of Crisis*. Cambridge, Mass.: Massachusetts Institute of Technology

EFQM (1994a). *EQA Application Brochure*. Brussels: European Foundation for Quality Management

EFQM (1994b). *Self Assessment Based on the European Model for Total Quality Management*. Brussels: European Foundation for Quality Management

Ford, R.N. (1969). *Motivation through Work Itself*. New York: American Management Associates

Hammer, M. and Champy, J. (1993). *Re-engineering the Corporation: a Manifesto for Business Revolution*. Brealey Publishing

Handy, C. (1989). *The Age of Unreason*. London: Business Books

Handy, C. (1994). *The Empty Raincoat*. London: Hutchinson

Herzberg, F.W. *et al.* (1959). *The Motivation to Work*. New York: John Wiley

Inter Company Productivity Group (1993). *Benchmarking the Supply Chain*. Bagshot: John Russell Associates Ltd

Juran, J.M. (1988). *Quality Control Handbook*. New York: McGraw-Hill

Katzenbach, J. and Smith, D. (1993a). 'The Discipline of Teams'. *Harvard Business Review*, March/April, p. 112

Katzenbach, J. and Smith, D. (1933b). *The Wisdom of Teams: the High Performance Organization*. Harvard: Harvard Business School Press

Lawler, E.E. (1992). *The Ultimate Advantage*. San Francisco: Jossey-Bass

Mahadevan, S. (1992) *Suggestion Schemes in BP Chemicals*. Internal Report, London

Maslow, A.H. (1954). *Motivation and Personality*. New York: Harper and Row

MBNQA (1992). *Submission Guidance Notes*. Washington, DC: Malcolm Baldrige National Quality Award

Mintzberg, H. (1993). *The Rise and Fall of Strategic Planning*. London: Prentice-Hall

Mullin, R. (1993). 'Re-engineering's Uneasy Guru Contemplates The Changes.' *Chemical Week*, 11 August, p. 40

Naj, A.K. (1993) 'Some Manufacturers Drop Efforts to Adopt Japanese Techniques'. *The Wall Street Journal*, 17 May

Napuk, K. (1993). *The Strategy-Led Business*. London: McGraw-Hill

Newstrom, J.W. and Davis, K. (1993). *Organizational Behaviour*. New York: McGraw-Hill

Oakland, J.S. and Followell, R.F. (1990). *Statistical Process Control*. Oxford: Heinemann Newnes

Peters, T. (1992). *Liberation Management*. London: Macmillan

Rank Xerox (1992). *EQA Submission Document*. London: Rank Xerox Ltd

Scott-Morgan, P. (1994). *The Unwritten Rules of the Game*. London: McGraw-Hill

Senge, P.M. (1990) 'The Leader's New Work – Building Learned Organisations'. *Sloane Management Review*, Vol. 32, No. 1

Senge, P.M. (1992). *The Fifth Discipline*. London: Century Business

Sheehy, P. (1993). *Inquiry into Police Responsibilities and Rewards*. Chairman's Report. London: HMSO

Thompson, P. (1990). *Sharing Success*. London: Collins

Troy, K.L. (1992). *Recognizing Quality Achievement: Non-cash Award Programs*. New York: Conference Board Report No. 1008

Walker Morris, J. (1973). *Principles and Practice of Job Evaluation*. London: Heinemann

Wright, V. and Brading, L. (1992). 'A Balanced Performance'. *TQM Magazine*, October, p 276

Index

ABB, 167
ABS Quality Evaluations Inc., 53
Acclaim, 38, 49
Achievement, 2, 3, 8, 14, 27, 29, 160, 165, 169, 177
Agenda:
  personal, 20, 88, 165
Alignment, 19, 23, 29, 42, 93, 105, 153, 164, 178
Allocation, 86
American National Standards Institute (ANSI), 40
Appraisal, 21, 42, 67, 98, 100
  bottom-up, 138
  example, 139
  formality, 137
  procedure, 134
  purpose, 142
  top-down, 137
Assessment:
  self, 113
Assumptions:
  hidden, 23, 64, 164
Awards, 38
  Baldridge, 40, 41, 52, 62, 112
  British Quality, 41
  Canadian Business Excellence, 41
  corporate, 51

European Quality, 28, 41, 51, 52, 62, 112
Excelsior, 41

Baldridge Award, 40, 41, 52, 62, 112
Band progression, 96
Barclays Bank, 56
Barriers, 22, 29, 34, 44, 47, 61, 85, 159
BBC, 56
Behaviour, 132
  absolute standards of, 132
  and culture change, 4, 6, 17, 18
  and differentials, 79
  and performance related pay, 89
  and recognition, 173
  and reward, 173
  barrier to recognition, 46
  defining dozen, 171
  essential, 133, 135, 171
  leadership, 25
  team, 29, 30
Benchmarking, 124, 127, 161, 162
Beneficial loans, 13
Best in class, 124, 125, 128
Boffins, 155
Bonuses, 13, 71, 99, 100
Bournville, 15

BP Chemicals, 7, 15, 17, 28, 60, 102, 119, 135
British Airways, 28, 56, 61
British Oxygen, 28
British Rail, 61
British Standards Institute (BSI), 40, 53
British Telecom, 28, 56
BS 5750, 40, 51, 53
BTR, 167
Bureau Veritas, 53

Cadbury, Thomas, 15
Cash:
 bonuses, 71
 recognition, 15
Casual recognition, 34
Cars:
 allocated, 13, 77
Celebration, 36
Cells:
 production, 157
Change, 4, 6, 74
 agents, 17, 90
 coaching, 172
Child care, 78
Circles:
 quality, 24, 161
Citizen's Charter, 41
Command and control, 7, 34, 159, 167
Commendation, 35
Commission, 72, 75
Committed, 86
Communication, 59, 77, 172
Community, 119
Comparisons, 85, 129
Competencies:
 essential, 153
Confidentiality, 85, 174
Contribution, 2, 8, 14, 164, 165, 177

Core:
 essential, 168
Cost:
 improvement, 7
 of living, 68, 97
 of quality, 87, 112, 129
 reduction, 7
Culture, 45, 46, 55, 87
 change, 2, 4, 6, 9, 17, 25, 167
 thrust, 16, 90
Customer, 5, 25, 40, 68, 75, 89, 116, 162, 169

Defect measures, 129
Delegation, 172
Det Norske Veritas, 53
Deming, W. Edwards, 40, 47, 59, 63, 113
Differentials, 72, 79
Directors, 74
Disorganization, 167
Downsizing, 7, 163

Eccentrics, 157
Empowerment, 6, 8, 101, 167
European Quality Award, 28, 41, 51, 52, 62, 112
Evaluation, 79, 94
Experience curves, 128

Fair, 85, 86
Fixers, 6
Formality, 137
Frustration, 2

Gainsharing, 74, 76, 102
GEC, 56
General Electric, 63, 76
Gifts, 36

Goals, 2, 9, 19, 24, 29, 55, 85, 168
  setting, 130

Health insurance, 13, 78
Hertzberg's theory, 11
Hierarchy, 7, 8, 23, 34, 155, 159, 167
  of acclaim, 38, 49
Honda, 28

IBM, 154
ICI, 61
Ideas, 2, 5
Improvement, 4, 15, 25, 59, 68, 70, 162, 174
Incentives, 74
Income:
  improvers, 69, 96
Individuals, 20, 30, 34, 38, 42, 58, 83, 91, 170
Innovation, 21
Inputs, 120
International Standards Organization (ISO), 40
Investors in People, 119, 154
Involvement, 62, 64
ISO 9000, 40, 51, 53

Japan, 8, 9, 28
Jargon, 163
JIT (just-in-time), 161
Job:
  enrichment, 2
  evaluation, 79, 94
  for life, 8
  knowledge, 79
  ownership, 3
  tenure, 21
  whole, 70, 170
Journalism, 35

Judgement, 83

Kaizen, 61, 128
Kanban, 161
Key performance indicators, 127, 128

Leadership, 18, 25, 28, 29, 158
Learning, 22, 25, 152, 153
  continuous, 154, 169, 174
  on-the-job, 155
  organizations, 153, 157
Lever, William, 15
Leyland Trucks, 167
Life insurance, 78
Listening, 172
Lloyds Register QA, 53
Local relevance, 90
Long-term benefits, 78
Loyalty, 8, 73, 169

Manager:
  front-line, 6
  middle, 6, 46, 168
Management style, 15, 47
Marumara, 77
Maslow's theory, 11
Measurement, 83, 85, 90, 111
Membership, 174
Mementoes, 36
Metrics, 127
Monsanto, 76
Morale, 2
Mortgage assistance, 13
Motivation:
  and differentials, 79
  and structure, 8
  and suggestion schemes, 62, 64
  and the fruits of reward, 165
  by change, 5, 6

Motivation, *cont'd.*
　by upward appraisal, 7
　in contracted-out functions, 169
　inherent, 1
　in teams, 26
　of long-term benefits, 79
　of recognition, 15
　or reward, 14, 66
Motorola, 11, 76, 123, 154
Multi-skilling, 3, 70, 157, 170

Nissan, 28, 63, 98, 134, 136

Objectives, 9, 10, 45, 67, 85, 89, 168
Outputs, 113
Outsourcing, 169
Overtime, 3, 68
Ownership, 3, 25, 174

Pay, 66, 68, 93
　as a motivator, 11, 67
　at risk, 72, 101
　by-age, 8, 71
　performance related, 69, 72, 82, 88, 159
　service, 71, 96, 99
　skill-based, 70
Peer group, 47
Pension schemes, 13, 78
Performance, 16, 82, 84, 96, 99
　key indicators, 127, 128
　measurement, 111–149
Perks, 77
Policy, 8, 29, 164, 174
　deployment, 9, 21
　pay, 16, 18
Port Sunlight, 15
Prevention, 5, 58

Price:
　of Conformance, 87, 112, 129
　of Non-conformance, 87, 112, 129
Privileges, 36, 78
Process, 4, 5, 45, 112, 120, 152, 162
　capability, 122
　control, 124
　key business, 45, 120, 121, 125, 127, 164
Productivity, 59, 64, 74, 75
Profit sharing, 13, 73, 105
Promotion, 8, 16, 39, 77
Public services, 85
Publications, 3, 5

Quality:
　Assurance (QA), 40, 53, 124
　circles, 24, 161
　cost of, 87, 112, 129
　management, (*see* Total Quality Management (TQM & TQ))
　six sigma, 123

Rank Xerox, 28, 62
Ratings, 147
Rationalization, 7
Recognition:
　agent for change, 17
　avoiding oversight, 50
　bonuses, 72
　casual, 34
　corporate, 39
　definition, 13
　in learning organization, 155
　key motivator, 12
　link to success, 16
　place for, 8
　process reinforcer, 5
　relationship to reward, 18, 42

INDEX

Recognition, *cont'd.*
  starting out, 49
  structured mechanisms, 37
  teams, 22, 26, 28
Re-engineering, 7, 163
Restrictive practices, 3
Restructuring, 7
Results, 42, 71, 75, 86, 89, 100
Reward:
  agent for change, 17
  bonuses, 72
  definition, 13
  for skill, 157
  fruits of, 165
  in learning organization, 155
  key motivator, 12
  link to success, 16
  package, 11, 27, 108, 175
  pay and value, 66
  performance related, 69, 72, 82, 88, 159
  place for, 8, 164
  policy, 16, 18, 67, 84
  targets, 67
  teams, 22, 26, 28
Rightsizing, 7
Rockwell, 76
Rolls-Royce, 28
Root cause, 5, 58
Rover, 28
Rucker, A. W., 74, 102

Salary, (*see* Pay)
Sales offices, 50
Satisfaction:
  customer (*see* Customer)
  employee, 117, 158, 168
Scanlon, J. N., 75, 102
Semaphore, 173

Service:
  payments, 71, 96, 99
  professions, 83, 85
SGS Yarsley, 53
Share:
  options, 13, 73, 107
  schemes, 13, 73, 106
Short-termism, 21, 88, 152
Shifts, 24, 37
Six sigma, 123
Skill, 24, 38, 70, 79, 89, 96, 99, 157
Small is beautiful, 166, 168
Social attitudes, 3
Soft issues, 134
Southern Water, 56
Specialists, 51, 155
Stakeholders, 73, 115, 162, 174
Standards, 40, 41, 72, 168
  absolute behavioural, 132
Status, 6, 8, 28, 39
  symbols, 77
Strategy, 9, 10, 67, 169
Structure, 4, 7, 8, 45, 79
  future, 166, 178
  trefoil, 168
Subsidiarity, 167
Subsidized meals, 13, 78
Success:
  links to, 16
Suggestion schemes, 3, 37, 56, 77,
    and TQM, 59, 62, 63
  Association of, 56
Sumitomo Rubber, 28
Sun Alliance Insurance Group, 56
Survival, 7

Tax, 13
Teams, 9, 20, 22, 28, 34, 42, 58, 62, 79, 83, 87, 91, 99, 153, 169, 171

Teams, *cont'd.*
  and TQM, 25
  self-managed, 25, 169
Teamwork, 28, 62, 77, 83, 87, 91, 169
Time rates, 94
Tokens, 36
Toyota, 28
Total Quality (TQM/TQ) 9, 17, 19, 34, 51
  and dangers of PRP, 88
  and measurement, 111
  and PRP, 87
  and suggestion schemes, 56, 59, 62, 63
  and teams, 25
  continuum, 161
  definition, 162
  failure of, 152
  links to reward, 87
  progress of, 112

Trade Unions, 15, 59, 70, 74, 98
Training, 18, 70, 147, 154
Twin citizenship, 167

Unemployment, 177

Value, 2, 16, 18, 57, 66, 98, 117, 168
Value added, 2, 55, 120, 121, 161
Vickers, 28
Virgin Group, 167
Vision, 19, 157, 169

Wages, (*see* Pay)
Wallace Co. Inc., 26
What and how, 89
Widows' benefits, 78
Work group, 28, 62, 161